Pedro Pérez Zeledón

Reply to the Argument of Nicaragua

on the question of the validity or nullity of the Treaty of Limits of April 15, 1858, to

be decided by the President of the United States of America

Pedro Pérez Zeledón

Reply to the Argument of Nicaragua
on the question of the validity or nullity of the Treaty of Limits of April 15, 1858, to be decided by the President of the United States of America

ISBN/EAN: 9783337402938

Printed in Europe, USA, Canada, Australia, Japan

Cover: Foto ©Suzi / pixelio.de

More available books at **www.hansebooks.com**

REPLY

ARGUMENT OF NICARAGUA

ON THE

QUESTION OF THE VALIDITY OR NULLITY OF THE TREATY OF LIMITS OF APRIL 15, 1858,

TO BE DECIDED BY

The President of the United States of America,

AS ARBITRATOR.

FILED ON BEHALF OF THE GOVERNMENT OF COSTA RICA

BY

PEDRO PÉREZ ZELEDÓN,

ITS ENVOY EXTRAORDINARY AND MINISTER PLENIPOTENTIARY
IN THE UNITED STATES.

(TRANSLATED INTO ENGLISH BY J. I. RODRIGUEZ.)

GIBSON BROS., PRINTERS AND BOOKBINDERS
1887.

CONTENTS.

iv

PAGE.

INTRODUCTION.

INTRODUCTION.

Two are the questions submitted to the arbitration of the President of the United States of America under the treaty of Guatemala of December 24, 1886. One, which is the principal, refers to the treaty of limits between Costa Rica and Nicaragua, which was concluded on April 15, 1858, and to its validity or nullity. The other, which is supplementary, or secondary, refers to the interpretation to be given to certain points in the said treaty alleged to be doubtful.

It was stipulated in the treaty of arbitration that both questions should be simultaneously discussed and decided, upon such proceedings, and within such periods of time, as follows:

1st. Within ninety days, subsequent to the acceptance of the Arbitrator, the arguments and documents of the two parties should be filed.

2d. Within eight days, subsequent to the above, the arguments and documents of each party should be communicated to the other.

3d. Within thirty days, subsequent to the above, the reply of each party to the argument and documents of the other, should be submitted.

4th. Within a period of six months, and by only one and the same award, all the questions should be decided.

In spite of this, which under the provisions of the treaty of Guatemala is plain, the Republic of Nicaragua has reserved for some future time her argument upon the second supplementary question, and comes and says that she holds herself in readiness to submit that argument, when the principal question is decided, or when the Arbitrator declares that the opportunity to do so has arrived, by signifying his intention of entering upon the interpretation of doubtful points.

The defense of Nicaragua ought to have understood, from the unity of proceedings which, under the express provisions of the treaty of Guatemala, characterizes the present arbitration, that the periods of time granted to both parties for the filing and answering the arguments on the two questions were not double, but simple; and that the two questions should be discussed together and decided at the same time by one and the same award.

The text of the treaty of arbitration is so extremely plain in this respect that the division attempted by Nicaragua cannot be satisfactorily explained. But, whether explained or not, the fact is that it cannot be allowed, because Nicaragua would then enjoy, in the present discussion, an undue advantage over Costa Rica, by being permitted to make her argument and exhibit her documents, at such time before the decision as might be suitable to her purposes, while Costa Rica would be deprived of the right of reading and refuting, at the time provided for by the treaty, the arguments and proofs of her opponent.

The treaty of arbitration plainly states that the first period of the debate, and no other, is the one wherein the briefs and evidence of either party should be filed. Neither of them can pretend to enjoy other and different opportunities, in regard to time, or otherwise, as are granted by the treaty.

The Government of Costa Rica has never entertained any doubt as to the construction to be placed upon the treaty of limits, the language of which seems to it, and to everybody else not prejudiced, to be perfectly plain. And yet, acting with that sincerity which becomes a controversy of this kind, it has not hesitated to frankly express its own opinion upon all the questions which the Government of Nicaragua propounded.

But the Nicaraguan Government, after presenting the strange doubts which occurred to it, and formulating them by means of extremely brief propositions difficult to understand, instead of explaining them as frankly and extensively as required, within the time in which such a thing was possible, now comes and says that it will enter into such explanations afterwards, at such moment as may be pleasing to it, or suitable to its purposes.

The Government of Costa Rica refuses its assent to any change or alteration in this way by the Nicaraguan Government of the provisions of the treaty of Guatemala.

I must say, also, a few words in regard to another point, of no less importance, referring to the distinction necessarily to be made between the questions which are the exclusive subject of the present arbitration and another different question which may eventually arise hereafter. The questions submitted to the present arbitration are, in substance, WHETHER THE *treaty of April* 15, 1858, *is or is not valid, and* WHAT *is the construction to be placed upon some of its provisions?* The other question —an essentially different one,—not actual, but potential or eventual,—which will never arise except in case that the treaty of 1858 is adjudged void,—which is not, by any means, before the Arbitrator,—and which, if it ever comes up, will come up in a form and on terms not yet agreed upon by the two Republics,—is to find out WHICH were the *respective territorial limits of the two countries prior to* 1858.

In other words, the question now under discussion is not "WHICH were the territorial limits of Costa Rica and Nicaragua prior to 1858?" but simply to determine the validity or invalidity of the treaty concluded on the 15th of April, 1858, for the purpose of fixing the frontier between the two Republics.

Whatever has been said, or may be said, by either party in regard to limits prior to 1858 has to be considered only as historical illustrations, but never as a matter of direct, immediate, and actual concern.

No opportunity exists at present to pass judgment upon the strength and efficiency of the Royal Ordinances and Letters-Patent of the Crown of Spain, speaking of limits between Costa Rica and Nicaragua, or to decide the questions of public law arising out of the incorporation of Nicoya into Costa Rica, in 1824, approved by the Federal Power and accepted by Nicaragua by her first Constitution.

Those matters will be amply discussed at the proper time, if the opportunity to do so should ever present itself; and then both Governments shall file such documents as may support, respectively, their different conclusions.

To decide the question of the day, the only one before the Arbitrator, as Nicaragua pretends, upon bases which cannot be established solidly without a previous and thorough knowledge of the ancient limits, would be to answer in advance a question which has not been submitted, nor presented or debated. It would be to prejudge the question without sufficient knowledge of the subject. It would be to involve, at the risk of nullity, things which the parties to the arbitration themselves distinctly separated in the treaty signed by them at Guatemala.

The Government of Costa Rica entertains the firm confidence that neither the tendency shown by the argument of Nicaragua to involve and confuse those questions will find any encouragement in the righteous and enlightened mind of the Arbitrator, nor that Costa Rica will be refused full defense of her rights, and absolute and strict equality with Nicaragua.

PART FIRST.

PART FIRST.

HISTORICAL ANTECEDENTS.

CHAPTER I.

LIMITS OF THE ANCIENT PROVINCE OF NICARAGUA.

THE present chapter, as well as the one following, in both
of which the frontiers of Costa Rica and Nicaragua, prior to
the treaty of April 15, 1858, are defined, might, without any
impropriety, be eliminated from the present reply, because, as
it has been said in the introduction, such is not the subject of
this controversy. But wishing, on the one hand, not to leave
any portion of the argument of Nicaragua unanswered, and
thinking, on the other hand, that it is in the interest of Costa
Rica to show that the treaty of 1858, far from enlarging her
territorial rights, actually abridged them, it has been deemed
necessary to devote a portion of this paper, as was done in the
former one, to some historical considerations, which, although
relating to matters not the subject of the arbitration, are, nevertheless, conducive, as it cannot be doubted, to the illustration
of the question at issue.

The defense of Nicaragua has confused two questions which
the treaty of arbitration distinguished with particular clear-
ness, and the interrogatory, "which were the ancient limits
of the Province of Nicaragua?" constitutes a cardinal basis
of her argument. In answer to that interrogatory she has
confined herself to simple assertions, supported only by incomplete and extremely compendious quotations from several Royal
Ordinances and from different writers; but no document em-
anating from the sovereign has been filed which shows what
the limits were during the Spanish rule.

It is asserted by the defense of Nicaragua that the Desaguadero or San Juan river belonged *ab initio* to that Republic: but this assertion is not correct, either legally or historically. Before refuting it, I must, however, be allowed to call attention to the change of basis which is noticed in that defense.

When Señores Don Tomás Ayón and Don Anselmo H. Rivas, Ex-Secretaries of Foreign Relations of Nicaragua, spoke for that Republic and defended her, the Desaguadero and the San Juan river were not one and the same thing; and the San Juan river had no more than one mouth; and the Desaguadero was situated in the Matina valley far south of the Colorado river. [1]

Now that the defense of Nicaragua is entrusted to other hands, the Desaguadero is the same as the San Juan river; it has not one but three mouths; and the frontier of Costa Rica is not to be found in the Matina valley, but on the right bank of the mouth of the Colorado river. [2]

Such variety and indecision in regard to such a capital point plainly reveal that Costa Rica has always had reason on her side; and that Nicaragua, much against her will, sees herself compelled now to acknowledge it, at least, by plainly confessing that their Secretaries of State who shouldered the burden and responsibility of expounding and defending her rights, committed an error.

The truth is that the Desaguadero is the same as the San Juan river, and that, although the waters of this stream have several outlets into the Atlantic, the historical and commercial mouth *par excellence*, the one recognized by the discoverers of the river, fortified during the colonial regime, the thoroughfare of traffic in the last years of that period, the vehicle of Central American commerce from the Independence up to some years subsequent to the treaty of 1858, when the port of San Juan became deteriorated, was always the mouth

---

[1] See pages 40 and 41, Argument of Costa Rica.
[2] Argument of Nicaragua.

of the northern branch of the river, the one properly named San Juan or Desagnadero, denominations which were never given either to the Taure or the Colorado rivers, known, both of them, in this century, as they were in the two preceding, by their own special names.

The San Juan river belonged ab initio *to Veragua and not to Nicaragua, but afterwards it was common to both Provinces.*

Had the King of Spain wished that Costa Rica should enjoy the San Juan river, he would have forbidden her to navigate it in the navigable portion thereof, would have eliminated it from her jurisdiction, and would have adjudicated it to Nicaragua to the exclusion of Costa Rica. But he did exactly the contrary, and the title in which Charles V mentioned the Desagnadero as being within the limits of Cartago, or Costa Rica, is precisely the one in which, for the first time, Nicaragua was given a right in the upper part of that stream. So it is, that closely following the language of the laws, or Royal Ordinances, of Emperor Charles V, and placing upon them the right construction, the territory of the lower part of the San Juan river belonged to Costa Rica, and the navigation of it and of the Lake was common to Costa Rica and Nicaragua. That community existed in law and in fact under the Government of the Federal Republic of Central America, and subsequent to it, also, when Nicaragua and Costa Rica organized themselves as independent Republics. It lasted until April 15, 1858, in which Costa Rica deemed it advisable to renounce a portion of her rights in favor of Nicaragua.

In proof of these assertions Costa Rica exhibits the statutes which fixed her territorial demarcation, and are clear and precise and emanate from the sovereign power. She also cites authorities of other kinds, as geographers and historians, but only when they corroborate or illustrate the legal provisions, not when they are in opposition to them, or contradict them without foundation, or err to the extreme of asserting one thing in one page and denying it in another. Costa Rica rejects the authority of the celebrated historian Antonio de Herrera, when that writer is found in palpable and unjustifiable contradiction with a Royal Ordinance. With much more reason she refuses to give credit to the assertions of Señor Don Tomás Ayón when they are not duly backed by authentic documents of as high authority as is required, for Señor Ayon's citations are incomplete, and his historical work abounds in material errors and inexplicable oversights.

Costa Rica pays respect to the law, to the law alone, and exhibits the text thereof, which is her title; while Nicaragua exhibits no title, and confines herself in her argument to cite such fragments from the titles of Costa Rica as she deems favorable to her pretension.

No one knows, therefore, what are the titles which Nicaragua has invoked for more than half a century; and we are forced to fill, to a certain extent, the void which she has left in her argument.

Gil Gonzalez Dávila discovered Nicaragua and made his first exploration between January, 1522, and May, 1523. He started from Panamá on January 15, 1522, and returned in June, 1523. But as soon as Pedrarias Dávila knew of his discovery he wanted to appropriate to himself the fruits thereof, and began to persecute Gil Gonzalez, who succeeded, however, in placing himself in safety by sailing to San Domingo.

Pedrarias commissioned Francisco Hernandez de Córdoba, the Captain of his Guard, for the conquest of the country discovered by Gil Gonzalez *to the west of Panamá on the Southern Sea*. Córdoba landed on the eastern shore of the Gulf of Orotina, or Nicoya, and founded the town of Bruselas in the early part of 1524. He proceeded in his voyage towards the Province of Nicaragua, and he succeeded so well that on May 1, 1524, he had reached the vicinity of Chinandega, where he distributed the booty and granted " encomiendas," or repartimientoes of Indians to his companions, not, however, without first apportioning more than one thousand of the same Indians to his chief Pedrarias, at the place of

Los Desollados. It was in the same year that he founded the cities of Leon and Granada, and sent Hernando de Soto to explore the country in the direction of Honduras.

In 1525 he fortified himself at Granada, and relying upon the eventual support of Cortés, who was then at Honduras, rebelled against the authority of Pedrarias, who, being informed by Hernando de Soto of the defection of his lieutenant, left Panamá in January, 1526, and went to punish him, as he did in the middle of that year, by causing him to be tried and put to death at the public square of Leon.

Absolute master of Nicaragua, but deprived of the Government of Castilla del Oro, Pedrarias succeeded in being appointed Governor and Captain-General of Nicaragua. His commission, which was issued on June 1, 1527, is at the same time the title or charter of the Province of Nicaragua, then created by it as a dominion of the Spanish crown.

Emperor Charles V did not define the precise boundaries of the new Province, which, as the Royal Patent reads, comprised

" the lands and provinces of the South Sea coast, towards the west, discovered and conquered by Francisco Hernandez de Córdoba, who, under your commission, settled in the Province of Nicaragua."

Said Royal Patent further reads:

" It is our mercy and will, that you, Pedrarias Dávila, during our pleasure, be invested with the Governorship and Captaincy-General of said lands and Provinces of Nicaragua." [1]

In subsequent royal ordinances and commissions, such as the one issued at Toledo on May 4, 1534, in favor of Rodrigo de Contreras, in which this Governor was vested with the same faculties as Pedrarias, no demarcation is made of the territory of Nicaragua; [2] but from the commission of Pedrarias and the royal ordinance of April 21, 1529, it can

---

[1] TORRES DE MENDOZA. *Colección de documentos inéditos*, vol. xl, p. 252, where the commission is found *in extenso*.

[2] TORRES DE MENDOZA. *Colección*, vol. XLI, page 521.

be seen that the authority of the Governors was to be exercised over the land conquered by Hernandez de Córdoba, from the town of Bruselas and the territory adjacent thereto, to the Honduras boundary. As has been said in the argument of Costa Rica, page 22, this territorial jurisdiction was gradually diminished by the creation of the new Provinces of Cartago, or Costa Rica, and Nicoya, on the side of the Southern Sea. There is not a single commission, a single royal ordinance, extending the jurisdiction of Nicaragua, during the XVIth century, to the coast of the Atlantic Ocean, and Herrera is the first one who, at the end of the said century, spoke of said coasts as belonging to her.

A historical error is committed by saying that Columbus discovered Nicaragua in 1502 when he travelled along the coast from Cape Gracias á Dios to Cariay or to the San Juan river. In doing this he did not reach Nicaragua, nor New Granada[1] either, but he only went along the coast of *Veragua*. That coast was afterwards a part of Costa Rica, and lately of Nicaragua.

The demonstration of this truth is simple. Twenty years before the discovery of Nicaragua those coasts were known by the name of Veragua, from Cape Camaron to the Gulf of Darien or Urabá. When, in 1509, the Catholic King gave the Government of Veragua to Diego de Nicuesa, the limits assigned to that command were from Cape Gracias á Dios to the Gulf of Urabá, comprising all the present coasts of Nicaragua, Costa Rica, and Panamá. The Mosquito coast was, therefore, a part of Veragua; and the San Juan river or Desaguadero ran unknown through the middle of that Province of Veragua.[2]

---

[1] In his history of the Jesuits in New Granada (*Historia de los Jesuitas en Nueva Granada*), chap. I, the Colombian writer, Don José Joaquin Borda, says that Columbus discovered New Granada when he saw Cape Gracias á Dios at a distance. Señor Ayón is historically wrong in saying that Columbus discovered Nicaragua, although Cape Gracias á Dios is now a part of that Republic.

[2] NAVARRETE. *Coleccion de los Viajes, &c.*

TORRES DE MENDOZA. *Ubi supra.*

On Dec. 24, 1534, seven years after Nicaragua was raised to the rank of a Governorship and Captaincy-General, Emperor Charles V appointed Felipe Gutierrez to be Governor of Veragua, and the limits of his territorial jurisdiction were from Cape Gracias á Dios to the boundary of Castilla del Oro.

In 1534 the Desaguadero was known to exist ; but neither it, nor the territory through which it flowed, were reserved for Nicaragua, that river continuing, therefore, to run entirely in the Province of Veragua.

In 1539 Captains Calero and Machuca explored its course and passed out through it to the Northern Sea ; and, although they fitted out their expedition at Granada under the auspices of Rodrigo de Contreras, they did not think to have discovered any unexplored part of the Government of Nicaragua, but an entirely new province, the Governorship of which they proposed to ask for Machuca. But before they had an opportunity to address the King, Doctor Robles, a justice of the recently established Audiencia of Panamá, under whose jurisdiction Nicaragua fell, gave commission to his son-in-law, Hernan Sanchez de Badajoz, to conquer Costa Rica, *from the limits of the Dukedom of Veragua up to Honduras,* thus including El Desaguadero, in the Province of Costa Rica. The Audiencia directed the Governor of Nicaragua to abstain from interfering in any manner with the said Province of Costa Rica, which was under another name, the same Government of Veragua[1] vacant by the failure of the expedition of Felipe Gutierrez and his flight into Peru.

The Governor of Nicaragua, feigning to be ignorant that the coast of the Caribbean Sea did not fall under his jurisdiction, paid no attention to the injunction of the Audiencia of Panamá, and, fitting out an expedition under his own command against

WASHINGTON IRVING. *Companions of Columbus.*

SIR ARTHUR HELPS. The Spanish Conquest of America, vol. 1, page 298 (with a map).

JUSTIN WINSOR. A Narrative and Critical History of America, vol. II (with maps), &c., &c. Boston. 1886.

[1] PERALTA. *Costa Rica. Nicaragua,* &c., pp. 89, 725, 747.

Hernan Sanchez de Badajoz, descended the Desaguadero and landed at Tariaca, now Talamanca (Costa Rica), where he arrested Badajoz and sent him as a prisoner to Spain.

In the eyes of the King, both Badajoz and Governor Contreras were guilty of usurpation, because neither of them had a direct commission from His Majesty to interfere with the government of Veragua, the appointment of whose superior authority depended exclusively upon the Crown, " because this is a matter which has to be treated only with our Royal Person and in our Council for the Indies."[1]

The King disapproved the appointment of Badajoz, made by the Audiencia of Panamá, and, by articles of agreement with Diego Gutierrez, of November 29, 1540, entrusted to the latter the government of Veragua on the same terms as it had been done with his brother and predecessor, Felipe Gutierrez. Veragua was given new limits, and named Cartago.

Those limits were from Rio Grande (River Aguan) and Cape Camaron to the Zarabaro Bay, comprising the Mosquito coast and the interior land, including the Desaguadero, to within fifteen leagues of the Lake of Nicaragua.

The King, by ordinance dated at Talavera on January 11, 1541, directed the Governor of Nicaragua, and all other authorities of the Indies, " not to meddle or intrude in the limits of the Government of Cartago;"[2] but Rodrigo de Contreras did not give up, and brought suit against Diego Gutierrez before the Council of the Indies, asking for himself alone the territory of El Desaguadero.

The Council decreed, in the last resort, what has been said, that is, that Gutierrez, by virtue of the agreement entered into with him, had the right to pass through the mouth of El Desaguadero, on the Northern Sea, and settle and allot reparti-

[1] Letters of the Council of the Indies to Doctor Robles, Associate Justice of Panamá, Madrid, April 24, 1540.

FERNANDEZ. *Colección de Documentos para la historia de Costa Rica*, Vol. iv, p. 76

[2] FERNANDEZ. *Ibidem*, page 102.

mientoes on both banks of that river up to within fifteen leagues of the lake. (See argument of Costa Rica, p. 32).

The Desaguadero was, therefore, an integral part of the Government of Cartago.

Diego Gutierrez made the Desaguadero the starting-point or centre of his expeditions. From there he went up as far as Granada in search of people and provisions; and from there he started for all the other places where he intended to establish colonies. In use of his faculties he appointed Francisco Calado Lieutenant Governor of El Desaguadero, and caused him to act at the same time as Treasurer of the Government.[1]

Upon the death of Gutierrez, which took place in the latter part of 1544, the Audiencia of Los Confines recommended the Council of the Indies to accede to the petition of Machuca, who wanted to be appointed Governor of El Desaguadero, or Costa Rica, which he had discovered; and the Bishop of Nicaragua made the same recommendation in favor of Alonso Calero. But as the son of Diego Gutierrez had the right to succeed his father in the Government of Cartago, and, by virtue of his faculties, had assigned and transferred his rights to Juan Perez de Cabrera, the latter, on February 22, 1549, obtained Royal letters investing him with the same right that Gutierrez had. Cabrera could not, however, owing to the opposition of the Audiencia of Los Confines, accomplish the conquest of Cartago; and in 1552 he obtained, in compensation thereof, the Government of Honduras.

During the time intervening between the death of Gutierrez and the expedition of Licentiate Cavallon to Costa Rica, in 1560, grave events took place in the other provinces of the Audiencia of Los Confines.

The tyranny of Rodrigo de Contreras was repressed in part by the Andiencia. He was put on trial and compelled to go to the

---

[1] Royal Letter of the Prince Governor (Philip II) to Diego Gutierrez.
PERALTA. *Costa Rica, Nicaragua*, &c., page 135.
BENZONI: *History of the New World*, Hakluyt Society, London, page 140.

Court to answer the grave charges preferred against him. The King heard the petitions of the Audiencia and Bishop Valdivieso, and the earnest request of Las Casas, and snatched the Province of Nicoya from the rapacity of the successors of Pedrarias Davila, who had kept it as a personal " encomienda." Nicoya was made a Corregidorship (Corregimiento), to be provided for by the royal crown ; and the Audiencia of Los Confines, or Guatemala, appointed the Corregidor thereof only temporarily until the King should act.

The reforms introduced by the Audiencia met with such a bad reception on the part of the Contreras, and so great was the anger caused on them by the loss of such a profitable " encomienda " as that of Nicoya, that they raised up in arms against the authority of the King. Hernando de Contreras, the son of the Governor of Nicaragua, killed, with his own hands, Bishop Valdivieso ; and his partisans, after this crime was accomplished, cried aloud in the streets, *Liberty ! long live Prince Contreras !*

The Contreras, however, expiated their folly with their lives.

The Governorship and Captaincy-General of Nicaragua was abolished, and Nicaragua became reduced to the rank of an "Alcaldia Mayor," whose head was sometimes appointed by the crown but oftener by the Audiencia of Guatemala. The creation of Nicoya as a " Corregimiento " was contemporary with the above said reduction of Nicaragua.

Nicaragua had to suffer again by a new revolt in 1554, and for eight years she bore the burden of ten "Alcaldes Mayores."

In the meantime the Province of Cartago remained without a Governor ; and the King, upon information of this fact, issued at Toledo the ordinances of December 13, 1559, and February 23, 1560, authorizing and instructing Licentiate Alonso Ortiz de Elgueta to conquer and people New Cartago, or Costa Rica, situated within the limits marked in the commission of Diego Gutierrez between Honduras and Nicaragua, comprising the Desaguadero and the whole land from sea to sea, as far as the jurisdiction of Tierra Firme on the side of Nombre de Dios and Panamá.

The King revoked the authority given Ortiz on February 5, 1561, before the latter left Spain, and directed the Audiencia of Guatemala to entrust the conquest of Cartago to Licentiate Cavallon, with the same powers as had been given to Ortiz. To facilitate his action Licentiate Cavallon had to be appointed Alcalde Mayor of Nicaragua. (Argument of Costa Rica, page 33).

Juan Vazquez de Coronado succeeded Licentiate Cavallon as Alcalde Mayor of Nicaragua and Costa Rica. He made a general exploration of the country east of the Gulf of Nicoya and sent Captain Francisco de Marmolejo to the southern shores of the Lake of Nicaragua and of the Desaguadero, inhabited by the Catapas, Tices, and Votos Indians, shores which Vazquez included in the Province of Costa Rica, although he was the Alcalde Mayor of Nicaragua.

The successors of Vazquez de Coronado, down to Diego de Artieda, exercised jurisdiction over the same territory, according to the Royal Ordinances and letters-patent of November 29, 1540, May 6, 1541, February 22, 1549, December 13, 1559, January 30, February 23, and July 18, 1560, February 5 and May 17, 1561, April 2, 1562, April 8 and August 7, 1565.[1]

These ordinances, enacted by the King of Spain upon consultation with the Council of the Indies, were the supreme law of the Monarchy in America; they all refer to one and the same territory; they all include the Desaguadero, as well as the bordering land, within the jurisdiction of Costa Rica, subject, however, to the limitations established by the articles of agreement of November 29, 1540, and the sentence of the Council of the Indies of May 6, 1541, and they are the earliest authentic titles

[1] PERALTA. *Costa Rica, Nicaragua y Panamá, &c.*, pp. 101, 113, 157, 175, 179, 181, 182, 194, 204, 378, 387.

LEON FERNANDEZ. *Colección de Documentos, &c.*, vol. iv, pp. 143 and 164.

TORRES DE MENDOZA. *Colección de Documentos Inéditos*, vols. xi, xiv, and xxiii.

which the ancient Provinces of Costa Rica and Nicaragua can invoke in support of their respective territorial rights in the region of El Desagnadero.

A perfect knowledge of these titles is indispensable to interpret correctly the articles of agreement signed at El Pardo on December 1, 1573, by King Philip II and Diego de Artieda, an instrument which might be called the territorial constitution of the Province of Costa Rica. (Argument of Costa Rica, p. 32).

There the limits of Costa Rica are marked, in the following language:

" The Province of Costa Rica and the other lands and provinces included therein, that is to say, from the North Sea as far as the South Sea in latitude, and in longitude from the confines of Nicaragua towards Nicoya, straight through the valleys of Chiriqui, as far as the Province of Veragua, on the south ; and on the north, from the months of the Desagnadero, towards Nicaragua, the whole territory down to the Province of Veragua."

This demarcation reduced the jurisdiction of Costa Rica· Charles V had extended it as far as the 16th degree of north latitude, and Philip II reduced it to the 11th degree. Under the former its northern extremity was Cape Camaron ; under the latter it was Punta de Castilla, as it is now.

It is evident that, in mentioning *the mouths of the Desagnadero*, the instrument does not simply allude to the place where the waters of the San Juan river empty into the sea, from where the coast should be followed in an imaginary line as far as Veragua. This would simply be to describe the length of the Atlantic littoral of Costa Rica. But the articles of agreement also speak of extent from the Northern to the Southern Sea, and refer to all the land that is included between the mouths of the Desagnadero and the Southern Sea. To go from those mouths towards the interior and find the Southern Sea, it is necessary to ascend the San Juan river until finding some place " *already taken* " by the Province of Nicaragua, as Article 5 of the instrument literally reads.

It is known that the Nicaraguan limit, on the east of the Lake, was within fifteen leagues of the latter, and did not comprise the Mosquito coast or the months of the Desaguadero; and no one has ever said, as the argument of Nicaragua pretends, that under the Artieda title, the Desaguadero *is entirely within the limits of Nicaragua.* Costa Rica maintains precisely the contrary. Nor has any one said, except Nicaragua, that El Desaguadero *belongs to Nicaragua in the whole of its course,* a proposition which is in flagrant contradiction of the literal language of the Royal Ordinances cited in the former argument of Costa Rica, and in the present reply, which cannot admit of the peculiar construction placed upon them by the argument of Nicaragua, unless by doing the greatest violence to grammar.

The Spanish expression, "á las partes de Nicaragua," does not mean "within the jurisdiction of Nicaragua," but "in the vicinity of Nicaragua," or "towards Nicaragua," or "on the side of Nicaragua." *A las partes, hácia, del lado,* of those Provinces, is not in Spanish to be *in them,* or *within them,* or *within their territory.*

"The mouths of the outlet, or Desaguadero, which is towards Nicaragua," does not mean that the Desaguadero is *in* Nicaragua, or *within* Nicaragua, but merely *near,* or *on the side of,* or *in the direction of,* or *towards* Nicaragua.[1]

This has been properly translated into English, in the argument of Costa Rica, "*towards Nicaragua,*" or as the Department of State did in Executive Document of the Senate, No. 50, 49th Congress, 2d session, "*near Nicaragua.*" And it may be translated also *to Nicaragua,* or *in the direction of Nic-*

[1] In reference to this point which, on the other hand is perfectly plain, see Syntactic Dictionary of the Spanish language (*Diccionario de Construccion y Régimen de la Lengua Castellana*), by R. J. Cuervo, *in verbo* "A," § 12, letter "A." "Enséñame, Aurelio, *a que parte* le dejaste." Cervantes. Galatea (Show me, Aurelius, *where* you left him). "*A todas partes* ve un ancho calabozo. Jovellanos. (He sees *everywhere* a broad calabose)." "**Tus abuelos** *á esta parte* habitaban. Reinoso (Your grandparents lived on this side).

aragua : but never *in,* or *inside,* or *within* Nicaragua, meaning inclusion in her territory.

That such an idea of inclusion is untenable is shown in two ways :

First, because the boundary, or terminal line, of Nicaragua towards the east, never reached, before 1573, the months of El Desaguadero ; and Artieda had authority under his title *to take possession in the name of the King of whatever was not already taken between* said mouths and the frontiers of Nicoya and the Southern Sea.

Second, because the same text of the Royal Grant in favor of Artieda, wherein the Spanish adverbial phrase *á la parte* occurs—once in singular with reference to the frontier between Nicaragua and Nicoya, and once in plural with reference to the location of El Desaguadero—shows that the construction placed upon it by Nicaragua, in the sense of inclusion, is absurd, because the boundary between Nicaragua and Nicoya could not be *inside of* or *within* Nicaragua. The most that can be said is, that it *was near her,* or *on her side ;* and in the same way, where it is said that El Desaguadero is *á las partes de* Nicaragua, that means only *towards* or *in the direction of* Nicaragua, but not *within* her territory.

The frontier of Nicoya, as recognized by the argument of Nicaragua, was the Del Salto river ; and not the mouth, or a single point thereof, but the stream itself, which separated Nicoya from the territory of the Chomes Indians. The Artieda agreement does not mention the Del Salto river ; but, while it is true that this river was one of the boundaries of the territory of the new Province, still there is no reason for saying that the Lake shore and the banks of the San Juan river were not limits of Costa Rica, since it appears that they had been taken possession of in the King's name by Juan Vazquez de Coronado, Perafán de Ribera, Don Gregorio de Sandoval, and other Governors of Costa Rica.

The instrument aforesaid admits of no other construction, and Nicaragua has not exhibited one single title to attenuate its strength.

The assertions of private writers, and the contents of maps representing the territorial jurisdiction of Nicaragua in a way different from the one shown by the titles of Costa Rica, do not deserve credit.

This is the case with the quotation from Mr. Squier in the argument of Nicaragua. The assertions of this writer have no foundation, either in law or in fact, and the dividing lines which he draws are purely imaginary. The Constitution of Costa Rica of 1825, to which he refers, understood the demarcation of Costa Rica to be the same as contained in the Articeda Royal grant, and could not exclude, nor did it exclude, from the Costa Rican territory the District of Bagaces and Las Cañas, situated on the banks of the Del Salto river, conquered by Vazquez de Coronado and subjected to the rule of Costa Rica in 1562.[1]

The Articeda agreement reads that the limits of Costa Rica begin on the side of the Southern Sea, from the place which they call of the Chomes Indians, from where the name of the Province, in the direction of Guatemala (*que cae á la provincia de Guatemala*), is derived, direct through the valleys of Chiriqui to the Province of Veragua.

It is to be noticed, in the above text, that the phrase, *que cae á la provincia*, which is herein translated, " in the direction of Guatemala," was used only to mean the course or direction, and not inclusion, since the Province of Los Chomes did not belong to Guatemala, and was more than one hundred leagues distant from it.

The Province of Los Chomes was situated on the left bank of the Del Salto river, and extended towards the interior as far as the source of the same river, and continued towards the south alongside the Gulf of Nicoya. It belonged to Costa Rica; its territory is the same as belonged to the ancient Province of Orotina; and the city of Aranjuez was founded in it by Perafán de Ribera, Governor of Costa Rica.

---

[1] PERALTA. *Costa Rica, Nicaragua, &c.*, pages 249, 401, 761, 766, 768.

The District of Nicoya ran along the right side of the Del Salto river, and included the peninsula of the latter name, extending itself to the north as far as the La Flor river and the shores of the Lake of Nicaragua.

It is true, and the argument of Costa Rica has so asserted, that Nicoya was, at one time, attached to the Government of Nicaragua ; but it is also true that the royal authority which could segregate it, or constitute it independent, did so segregate and constitute it.

When it is said, in the Cavallon's commission of "Alcalde Mayor" of New Cartago (cited in the argument of Nicaragua, page 10), that his territorial jurisdiction extended from the limits of the town of Nicoya, of the said Province of Nicaragua, further on, &c., it is not meant that Nicoya was under the jurisdiction of Nicaragua. This language was used in the way of an archaism, by considering Nicoya as a geographical or ethnological dependency of Nicaragua, as Portugal is of Spain. And the proof is that, precisely in that very year, 1561, in which the Audiencia of Guatemala issued Cavallon's commission, Nicoya was already independent from Nicaragua, as has been shown, and is witnessed by the Royal Ordinance of July 18, 1560, and by the letter of the Audiencia of Los Confines, to which the former was an answer.

The Audiencia writes from Guatemala, on the 18th of December, 1559, and uses this language :

" The Province of Veragua, otherwise called Nueva Cartago, is in this district ; which borders on the Province of Nicoya, where your Majesty has always one ' Corregidor' (Mayor), and where, for the past two years, certain neighboring Indians, called the Chomes, have been reduced to submission," &c., &c.

The King answers :

" You say that the Province of Veragua, otherwise called Nueva Cartago, is in your district and borders on the Province of Nicoya, where we have always a Corregidor. * * * For the purpose of peopling Nicoya and her neighboring country we have already instructed Licentiate Ortiz, our Alcalde Mayor of the Province of Nicaragua, and given him the proper authority."

It is evident that, if Nicoya should have been within the jurisdiction of the Alcalde Mayor of Nicaragua, no such special authority, as the one given Licentiate Ortiz, would have been required to govern it. When Licentiate Cavallon came to replace Ortiz, the former had not under his charge the Corregimiento of Nicoya which the Audiencia of Los Confines entrusted to Juan Romo. Vazquez de Coronado, the successor of Cavallon, in addressing the Corregidor of Nicoya, does not speak to him as to a subordinate, but as to an equal.[1]

The argument of Nicaragua states affirmatively that Señor Peralta has virtually admitted that Nicoya belonged to Nicaragua, because, in a note made by him in the text of the Articda agreement, he says:

"The Province of Nicoya was finally aggregated to Costa Rica in the year 1825."

But this phrase only means that the aggregation then made, had taken place other times before, and was then made for the last time. And so it is that Señor Peralta, in another note made by him in the agreement with Don Fernando de la Cueva (Costa Rica, Nicaragua y Panama, p. 148), uses the following words:

" Let it be noticed that by this agreement, as by the one with Diego de Articda, Nicoya was subject to the Governors of Costa Rica, and that her dependency from Nicaragua was scarcely anything else than nominal. When it was not governed by ' Corregidores' or 'Alcaldes Mayores' directly dependent upon the Crown, it was rather submitted to Costa Rica."

The Articda agreement reads as follows:

" 14. And, whereas, between *the Province of Nicoya* and the quarters which you are going to people, and where you will reside in the said Province of Costa Rica there must be a

---

[1] PERALTA. *Costa Rica, Nicaragua*, &c., pp. 178, 213, 221 to 224. Letters of the Alcalde Mayor of Nicaragua to Juan Romo, Corregidor of Nicoya.

great distance, and it is advisable that some person be appointed there to administer our justice and assist you in everything necessary or advisable, we do hereby give you the necessary authority to send a competent person to the said Province, who will be there your Lieutenant, at the salary of as many maravedises a year as have been paid to the former 'Corregidores' and 'Alcaldes Mayores' of the said Province," &c.

The agreement with Don Fernando de la Cueva, dated at Madrid on the 29th of December, 1593, is no less explicit. It reads as follows:

"Firstly. It is my will that you shall have the Governorship of the said Province of Costa Rica and the Alcaldia Mayor of Nicoya—the said Governorship for twelve years, and the Alcaldia Mayor for eight, as it was with Diego de Artieda Cherino," &c.[1]

If the Honorable Minister of Nicaragua would have fixed his attention on all the articles of the Artieda and Don Fernando de la Cueva agreements, especially Article 14 of the former, he would have convinced himself of the fact that Nicoya and Nicaragua were not one and the same political body —one and the same Province—but two independent entireties, as independent as they could be, under the same Sovereign and the same laws. Some branches of their government—as, for instance, the ecclesiastic and financial branches—were always common, and the superior chief was common to Nicaragua, Costa Rica, and Nicoya.

The argument of Nicaragua also says that, "according to the Artieda agreement, the Desaguadero completely falls within the limits of Nicaragua."

That was not the opinion of the legislator. Philip II believed to have given Costa Rica as its limits the *mouths* of the Desaguadero, and not the most southern one. Artieda had authority to occupy the three mouths, and keep them under the jurisdiction of Costa Rica.

---

[1] PERALTA. *Ubi supra*, pages 503 and 649.

The proof that *none* of the three mouths of the Desaguadero belonged to Nicaragua is furnished by the Royal Ordinance of Philip II of February 10, 1576, directing the Audiencia of Guatemala to enter into an agreement with Captain Diego Lopez to conquer and people the Province of Taguzgalpa, that is to say, the part of the old Government of Cartago which was not included within the limits given to Artieda.

The Audiencia entrusted Licentiate Diego Garcia de Palacio, one of its justices to enter into an agreement in the name of His Majesty with Diego Lopez. Article 1st of that agreement reads as follows:

" Firstly. His Majesty will appoint him his Governor and Captain-General for the said Province, which is all the land included between the mouth of the Desaguadero and the Camaron Point on the northern side, where the Province of Honduras begins; and from there towards the interior, the whole territory ending at what is now the limit of the jurisdiction of the Province of Nicaragua and Nueva Segovia, and also of Honduras."[1]

From the documents and facts above alluded to it appears to be evident that in 1576 the Province of Nicaragua did not exercise any jurisdictional rights over the mouths of the Desaguadero, or over the coasts on the Atlantic side ; and that consequently the interpretation given by Nicaragua to the Artieda agreement is erroneous.

Nicaragua never established any colony on the southern bank of the San Juan river which was never occupied by her. On the northern bank she founded Jaen, on the outlet of the Lake, at the place where Fort San Cárlos now stands. The southern bank was considered to belong to Costa Rica, and when the fortress, which is now called Castillo Viejo, was

---

[1] See Document No. —.

TORRES DE MENDOZA. *Colección.* Vol. xiv, p. 528, where the document *in extenso* is found.

PERALTA. *El Rio San Juan de Nicaragua* in Executive Document of the Senate, No. 50, 49th Congress, 2d Session, page 38.

built on the Costa Rican bank of the San Juan river, the one
who ordered the work to be done and superintended it was not
the Governor of Nicaragua, but the Captain-General of Guatemala, who exercised high jurisdictional rights over Costa
Rica. The work was done at the expense of the Treasury of
the Royal Audiencia, and under the technical inspection of the
" Adelantado " of Costa Rica, Don Juan Fernandez de Salinas.

In the time of the Spanish Government the San Juan river
belonged as much to Costa Rica as to Nicaragua; and the in-
nocent use and defense thereof against any foreign enemy
were, respectively, a right and a duty of the two provinces. The
free navigation and commerce through that river was not an
exclusive favor granted to Nicaragua, but a benefit bestowed
upon the two riparian provinces, in order not to compel them
to export their products by the far distant ports of Omoa and
Trujillo in Honduras.

The same status of community of use and nationality of the
San Juan river was retained during the Government of the
Federal Republic of Central America; and the illustrious
President Morazan was the one who, in the name of the common
country, and not of Nicaragua alone, or of Costa Rica, wanted
to make it serve the progress of the world and the common
good of Central America, by directing, in 1837, John Baily,
an English engineer, to make that exploration of the San Juan
river, the Lake, and the Rivas Isthmus for the purposes of
an interoceanic canal, which became famous. The Federal
Republic of Central America, not the State of Nicaragua, took
steps in that direction and entered into a favorable contract
with the King of Holland for the opening of that canal.

It was Costa Rica who, in later times, gave the mortal blow to
William Walker, by occupying with her forces the river banks,
and seizing the transit steamers which carried provisions and

¹ Decrees of the Federal Congress of Central America of June 16, 1825,
and October 21, 1830.

Dunlop. Travels in Central America, London, 1847, pp. 31 and 35.

Squier. Nicaragua, New York, 1856, vol. ii, pages 253, 257, 259.

reinforcements for that leader. It was Costa Rica who captured Castillo Viejo and who compelled Walker to capitulate.

What moved Costa Rica to throw herself into the struggle? It was not a Quixotic love of war nor a vain ambition for glory. It was the common danger, the defense of the common soil, the powerful feeling of solidarity which in times of difficulty causes sister nations to forget their former quarrels and secure, by means of their united efforts, the liberty of the common country.

This community in danger, and in the duty of self-defense, implied common and equal rights in the navigation of the San Juan river which Costa Rica reclaims with justice.

THE natural limits of Costa Rica are those of the *uti possi-detis* of 1826, from the mouth of the San Juan river, and following the thalweg or mid-channel of the same, and continuing through the Lake of Nicaragua in a straight line up to the mouth of the Sapoá river on the same Lake, to the mouth of the La Flor river on the Pacific Ocean. This boundary is the one which Mr. Squier called " pretended boundary of Costa Rica in 1850." In the copy of the map of Squier appended to the argument of Nicaragua this line has been omitted.

" Pretended boundary of Costa Rica " is not a correct expression. Mr. Squier would have expressed himself with much more propriety if he had said " actual boundary of Costa Rica *disputed by Nicaragua*." Nor is it correct, either, to state that Costa Rica, in 1850, *pretended* a boundary, which ever since 1825 had been marked out by decree of the Federal Congress enacted on December 9th of that year. It is still less correct to state that the limits of Costa Rica are those set forth by her Constitution of January 21, 1825, because the article of that Constitution which refers to limits (Art. XV) was virtually reformed and amended by the Federal Congress. Those very same limits spoken of as *pretended* in 1850 were the ones set forth by the decree of Bases and Guarantees of March 8, 1841, and by the Costa Rican Constitution of April 9, 1844, and by all the statutes enacted in Costa Rica subsequent to January 25, 1825, for the organization of the District of Nicoya. Therefore, whatever has been said in this respect by Mr. Squier lacks foundation in fact.

Prior to Mr. Squier, the celebrated traveller, John L. Stephens, had been in Central America in the capacity of Chargé de Affaires of the United States. He visited Costa Rica in the early part of 1840. In chapter XVIII of his *Incidents of Travel in Central America, Chiapas, and Yucatan*, expresses himself as follows :

" At dusk we reached the river which runs by the suburbs of Guanacaste, the frontier town of Costa Rica."

Further on he says :

" I did not wish to continue on the direct route to Nicaragua, but to go first to the port of San Juan on the Pacific, the proposed termination of the canal to connect the Atlantic and Pacific Oceans. The commandant regretted that I had not come one day sooner. He mentioned a fact of which I was aware before, that Mr. Baily, an English gentleman, had been employed by the Government (of Central-America) to survey the canal route."

In another passage, wherein he refers to his remaining on the Santa Rosa estate, belonging to Don Juan José Bonilla, a Costa Rican gentleman, he says :

" The boundary line of the State of Costa Rica is a river (La Flor) in the midst of a wilderness, and he (Don Juan José Bonilla) was obliged to travel on horseback to Nicaragua (Rivas), a journey of four days."

Mr. John Baily, already named, and from whom Squier sometimes quotes (*Nicaragua*, Vol. II, page 231, &c.,) had a perfect knowledge of Central America. In 1823 he translated into English the *History of Guatemala* by JUARROS. . Fifteen years later he explored the line of the canal and travelled along the whole extent of the frontier of Costa Rica and Nicaragua. After residing 25 years in the country, whose history, laws, and topography were familiar to him, he published in London, in 1850, his book entitled *Central America*, with a map which Mr. Squier adopted and corrected in 1856, according to his own ideas and interests. In this work and map Baily gives Costa Rica, as her limits, from the mouth of the La Flor river to the mouth of the San Juan river, following the dividing line of the *uti possidetis* of 1826.

The learned Austrian traveller, Carl von Scherzer, who

visited Central America, by commission of the Imperial Academy of Vienna, at the same time as Mr. Squier, and in subsequent years, says :

" The Federation was dissolved in 1839, and since that time the State of Nicaragua has been an independent Republic, although with uncertain limits. The Province of Guanacaste, which formerly belonged to her, legally incorporated itself into Costa Rica ; but the right to the southern shore of the Lake of Nicaragua and to the right bank of the San Juan river remains in dispute, although *de facto* in the possession of Costa Rica."

" It may be said, under the present political condition of things, that the southern frontier of Nicaragua is the San Juan river, the southern shore of the great lake and the mountain which extends across the narrow Isthmus from the mouth of the Sapoá river to the Gulf of Salinas."[1]

Mr. Bedford Pim, an officer of the British Navy, who also visited the Republics of Costa Rica and Nicaragua twenty-seven years ago, and obtained from Nicaragua a railroad grant, is even more explicit than Scherzer, and, although writing after Squier, expresses himself as follows :

" The old boundary, by charter of 1574, commenced at the mouth of the river San Juan, and extended up that stream within fifteen leagues of the Lake, whence a line was drawn due west to the head-waters of the Rio Salto and down that stream to the Pacific. To the north and west of that boundary line lies the District of Guanacaste, which was annexed to Costa Rica after the independence by the free-will of the inhabitants in 1824, and their action was approved by the Federal Congress of Central America in 1825. Guanacaste has since then been in actual possession of Costa Rica, and its northern boundaries would, therefore, be those of Costa Rica, viz., the remaining fifteen leagues of the Rio San Juan, and now the entire length of that stream, thence along the borders

---

[1] SCHERZER. *Travels in the Free States of Central America.* 2 vols. London, 1857. Chapter ii, page 25.

of the Lake to the Rio Sapoá, and from the source of that stream to the beautiful harbor of Salinas Bay, on the Pacific."[1]

The quotations could be multiplied *ad libitum* to show what, in fact, needs no demonstration; that is, that the limits of Costa Rica, if those of the treaty of 1858 are rejected, are *de jure* and *de facto* those of the *uti possidetis* of 1826. But as Nicaragua, in her argument, has quoted from Squier and copied his map, Costa Rica has deemed it advisable to show that the opinions of Mr. Squier are not "the law and the prophets" among the authors.

Costa Rica, on the other hand, has shown that, besides the authority of the travellers and writers above cited, she has on her side the superior authority of both the laws and the geographic facts.

It is a self-evident geographical fact that the principal supply of the San Juan river does not come from the Lake of Nicaragua, although it is its outlet, but from the Costa Rican rivers, some of which are navigable, as the Frio, the San Carlos, and the Sarapiquí rivers.

The importance of the latter is such that Monsieur Paul Levy, a French engineer in the service of the Government of Nicaragua, in an official publication made by order and at the expense of that Government, and dedicated to Don Fernando Guzman and Don Vicente Quadra, two ex-Presidents of that Republic, says "that the San Juan river is no more than a tributary of the Sarapiquí."[2]

Mr. Thos. Reynolds, in a report addressed to President Cleveland and transmitted by him to Congress with his Message of the 5th of January last, corroborates the same remark in the following words:

"The great river of the central interoceanic valley of Central America is the Sarapiquí, and the Upper San Juan and

---

[1] BEDFORD PIM, R. N. *The Gate of the Pacific*, p. 24. London, 1863.
[2] LEVY. *Notas Geográficas y Económicas sobre la República de Nicaragua.* Paris, 1873, with a good map of Nicaragua.

the San Cárlos rivers are affluents to it, somewhat as the upper Mississippi is an affluent of the Missouri; but in the former case as in the latter the name of the less important of the two streams has been given to that formed by their junction. But even at the junction of the Upper San Juan with the San Cárlos the latter dominates in given characteristics to their combined waters, and where these fall into the still greater Sarapiquí those characteristics are intensified."[1]

The Sarapiquí river, as is well known, is exclusively Costa Rican, and it being the principal artery of the hydrographic system of the region of the San Juan river, it is just and logical to recognize that Costa Rica has the same rights of navigation as far as the sea, which the Government of Canada has in the St. Lawrence river. The Sarapiquí is navigable for about fifty miles, and between its confluence with the San Juan and the bifurcation of the latter to form the Colorado river, there are only thirteen.

The San Cárlos river is also exclusively Costa Rican, and in the rainy season is navigable for 60 miles. From its mouth on the San Juan river to the mouth of the Sarapiquí there are 25 miles, and to the bifurcation of the Colorado there are 38.

The Colorado river supplied more by the Pocosol, the San Cárlos and the Sarapiquí rivers, than by the scanty amount of water which flows from the Lake, runs exclusively through Costa Rican territory, in an extent of 20 miles to the Caribbean Sea, and is navigable for vessels drawing a large amount of water.

From the mouth of the Colorado river to the San Cárlos pier there are 118 miles navigable, 80 within the Costa Rican territory, and 38 on the San Juan river, on the part thereof whose right bank always belonged to Costa Rica.

Equity as well as international law, and the laws which created and organized the present Republics of Central America,

[1] Executive Document No. 57, House of Representatives, 49th Congress, 2d Session. *Condition and commerce of Nicaragua, Honduras and Salvador, p. 19*

recognize that Costa Rica has as much right as Nicaragua in the San Juan river.

The treaty of April 15, 1858 restricted and abridged considerably the rights of Costa Rica. If it falls, Costa Rica shall recover by the same fact her former limits, that is, the thalweg or mid-channel of the San Juan river to the Lake, thence a straight line to the mouth of the Sapoá river, thence another line to the La Flor river, and thence along the course of the latter to the Pacific Ocean. These are by all means the legal and natural limits of Costa Rica.

PART SECOND.

PART SECOND.

ELUCIDATION OF THE PRINCIPAL POINT.

CHAPTER I.

ARGUMENTS OF NICARAGUA AGAINST THE VALIDITY OF THE TREATY OF APRIL 15, 1858.

THE reasons set forth in the argument of Nicaragua, for the purpose of invalidating the treaty of limits of April 15, 1858, which that Republic concluded with Costa Rica, are three, to wit:

1st. That the treaty did not receive the sanction required by the fundamental law of Nicaragua for the perfection of a compact of its nature.

2d. That the treaty was not ratified by the Government of Salvador, and that the guarantee stipulated in favor of Nicaragua, as to Article X of that instrument, was not given effect.

3d. That the ratifications of the treaty were exchanged before it was submitted to the Congress of Nicaragua, and that the approval given by that Congress was subsequent to the expiration of the time agreed upon for that purpose.

From here it might be thought that the Government of Nicaragua has deemed it advisable to withdraw from the present discussion all the other reasons which, in its former correspondence with the Government of Costa Rica, at different times, it used to allege against the treaty,—reasons all of them, which were, in the belief that they would also be presented here, refuted at length in Chapters XI and XV of the Second Part of the "Argument" of Costa Rica.

But this silence, which certainly would have implied an admission of the groundless character of the reasons withheld, and simplified the discussion, is no more than apparent, because the omitted reasons are set forth again, although indirectly and incidentally, in the discussion of other points more or less related to them.

An additional reason has now been given—the one occupying the 3d place in the foregoing list—which Nicaragua never presented or thought of before, in spite of the many years which the debate has lasted.

Under the circumstances aforesaid I shall not be able to confine myself to a mere reply to the three reasons alleged by Nicaragua in support of her claim that the treaty of 1858 is void ; but I shall have to consider all other points indirectly maintained by her in order that none of her arguments, whether formally or informally presented, remain unanswered.

THE TREATY OF LIMITS WAS MADE IN STRICT PURSUANCE OF THE FUNDA-
MENTAL LAW IN FORCE IN NICARAGUA AT THE TIME OF ITS CONCLU-
SION.

THE first and principal reason alleged by the Government
of Nicaragua to deny the validity of the treaty of 1858, is because the said treaty did not receive the sanction required by
the fundamental law of the State for the perfection of a compact of its nature.

This assertion is wholly incorrect, as was shown by the former argument on behalf of Costa Rica, and as will be now
substantiated still more by the following considerations.

For the conclusion of the treaty of 1858, all the formalities
required by the public law of Nicaragua, in force at that time,
without the omission of a single one, were faithfully complied
with.

The regime which existed at that time in Nicaragua was
not the regular constitutional one which preceded the revolution initiated on May 5, 1854, and followed the Constitution
of August 19, 1858.

It was one, in every respect, exceptional and transitory, devoted above all to the political reorganization of the country.
Hence it was that the Executive concluded the treaty upon
bases given to it by the National Constituent Assembly, and
ratified it in use of faculties for that purpose delegated to it
by the Assembly; that the treaty was exchanged and promulgated as law of the Republic by virtue of the said ratification;
and that, in fine, it was not approved by the Assembly until
after the exchange of the ratifications. All of this might,
perhaps, have been done differently under circumstances of a
regular regime, not constituent but constitutional.

The defense of Nicaragua has forgotten completely what
was the political condition of its own country at the time in

which the treaty was initiated, negotiated, ratified, exchanged, promulgated, and carried into execution; and so it is no wonder that it reaches conclusions which it itself would have rejected if it had placed the question on its proper grounds.

To maintain that the condition of Nicaragua from May, 1854, to August, 1858, was a regular constitutional one, is tantamount to tearing from the history of that country, and of Central America in general, some of its most interesting pages, where the record has been preserved of the Nicaraguan civil struggles, the overthrow of the legitimate government, the usurpation of William Walker, the war waged by the five Central American States, at the head of which Costa Rica had the glory to present herself to snatch from the hands of the usurper his prey, and secure the common independence, and, finally, the advent of the dictatorial dumnvirate, which, "in spite of all predictions to the contrary, not only saved the country from the new struggle which threatened it, but wisely conducted it to its constitutional organization."[1]

The constitutional legality was represented in Nicaragua at the beginning of the revolution by the Government of General Chamorro and by the Constitution of 1854; but neither this Constitution nor the legitimate successor of General Chamorro's Government ever appeared again on the political stage of the country after peace was re-established.

The administration of General Martinez was simply an extraordinary one, which, although beneficial to the country which it helped to organize, had been born out of the revolution. The Constituent Assembly, also, was an extraordinary national representation, convoked by the dictatorial dumnvirate to reconstruct the country.

The Executive over which General Martinez presided and the National Constituent Assembly held in their hands, at the time when the treaty was made, all the powers required for the conclusion of the latter and for its perfection.

---

[1] GERÓNIMO PÉREZ. *Memorias sobre la revolución de Nicaragua.* Vol. ii, p. 215. See Document No. 52.

All that was enacted by the Constituent Assembly, and sanctioned and promulgated by the Executive, was law of Nicaragua. So it is witnessed by the statute-books of that country, where several enactments of this kind, respected and obeyed, both then, and now, as national laws, can be found without difficulty.[1]

To such an extent was the regime existing in Nicaragua at the time of the treaty of 1858 extraordinary, that the Constituent Assembly, by decree of December 10, 1857, decided to sanction and enforce in advance one chapter of the new Constitution (Chapter xvii), which defined the powers of the Executive. And this was done for the purpose that the Executive could enter at once, without waiting for the Constitution, which was not approved until August 19, 1858, and without finding obstacles of any kind, into negotiations with Costa Rica for the final adjustment of all differences in regard to limits, and thus secure that peace which was so desirable under those circumstances.[2] The defense of Nicaragua has also forgotten this fact.

The Constituent Assembly, besides acting in this way for the purpose that the differences with Costa Rica should be speedily and finally settled, enacted also a decree directing the Executive to continue the interrupted negotiations, and furnished it with certain bases for the conclusion of the treaty of limits, approving thus beforehand what might be done in accordance therewith.[3] This is another most essential fact which the defense of Nicaragua has not been pleased to remember.

The Executive carried out the instructions given by the Constituent Assembly, and as soon as it negotiated the treaty of 1858, in strict conformity to the bases suggested by that body, ratified, exchanged, and executed it, in use of its faculties.

---

[1] The files of the *Gaceta* of 1858 show no less than 103 laws passed by the Assembly, many of which were of fundamental character.
[2] See pages 71 and 72 of the Argument of Costa Rica of October 27, 1887.
[3] See page 73, Argument of Costa Rica of October 27, 1887.

The Constituent Assembly, having full knowledge of the facts which had been published in the official organ, and which the Executive had, furthermore, reported to it minutely, clothed the treaty with its approval. This approval, sanctioned likewise by the Executive, was also published as law of the Republic.[1]

The exceptional circumstances of political reconstruction, under which Nicaragua was, when the treaty of limits was made, satisfactorily explain why it was that the ratification of the treaty was made by the Executive, as delegate of the Constituent Power, and why the act of exchange followed, and did not precede, the approval by the Assembly.

But the defense of Nicaragua, besides ignoring all these circumstances, and avoiding to enter into any consideration thereof, has not hesitated to change their character by giving the name of " Constitutional Congress, or Assembly " to the Constituent body above mentioned. No law ever passed by that body fails to read in its heading, as can be seen in the statute-books, " The Constituent Assembly," &c.

So great is the desire shown by the defense of Nicaragua of avoiding to give the Constituent Assembly which approved the treaty its proper name, that even in the literal translation of the decrees of that body,[2] it has found it advisable to change that name into the one of " Constitutional Assembly," as if the English language had not the word " constituent," conveying the same idea as the Spanish word "constituyente," used in the Spanish text.

When the Assembly gave its approval to the treaty, the latter was already a Nicaraguan law. But that approval, although not intended principally to perfect it, because it was already perfect, added to its strength. Its principal object was to relieve the Executive from whatever responsibility that might arise out of the exercise of the faculties delegated to it for the conclusion and ratification of the compact.

---

[1] See page 55, Argument of Costa Rica of October 27, 1887.
[2] See Argument of Nicaragua of October, 1887, page

The approval, therefore, was nothing else than one of those corroborative acts which in the course of business often occur, and rest upon the well known and salutary principle *quod abundat non nocet*. If that approval had never been given, the validity of the treaty would not have been affected in the least.

The delegation of legislative powers, made in favor of the Executive, was not an act contrary to the public law of Nicaragua. Even under conditions of regular constitutional regime such a thing is perfectly legitimate in that Republic. (Article 42, section 25, Nicaraguan Constitution of 1858).

The public law of Nicaragua, applicable to the case, and in force at the time of the conclusion of the treaty of limits, was not, as claimed in the argument to which I now reply, the Constitution of 1838; but, on the one hand, Chapter XVI of the Constitution of 1858, promulgated in advance by special decree of December 10, 1857, and, on the other hand, the decree of the Constituent Assembly of February 5, 1858, providing for both the form and the substance of the treaty which was to be adjusted.[1]

No allegation has ever been made that the said laws, whose existence not even has been mentioned in the argument of Nicaragua, were violated. And if the treaty was made, as it was, in strict compliance with their provisions, nothing else is required to cause Nicaragua to respect it as one of her laws, as she did from 1858 to 1872, through her Legislative Congresses, her Executive Cabinets, and her officials of all kinds.

What was done by the President of Nicaragua, Don Tomás Martinez, within the legality of the circumstances, and by virtue of the faculties delegated to him by the Constituent Assembly, was entirely constitutional and lawful; and binding upon the nation.

Vattel says:

" If the nation has transferred the plenitude of sovereignty

---

[1] See page 73, Argument of Costa Rica of October 27th, 1887.

to its ruler, if it has trusted to him the care and vested in him the right, without reserve, of treating and contracting with the other States, it is deemed that it has vested it with all the powers necessary to render his contracts valid. The Prince (or the ruler) is then the organ of the nation; what he does is reputed to be done by it; and although he is not the owner of the public property he can alienate it validly."[1]

And that great luminary of the American law, Chancellor Kent, in discussing this subject, expresses himself as follows:

" If a nation has conferred upon its Executive Department, without reserve, the right of treating and contracting with other States, it is considered as having vested it with all the power necessary to make a valid treaty." [2]

And if the circumstance that the formalities of Article 194 of the Constitution of 1838 were not observed should ever produce as its result the nullification of the treaty, the inevitable conclusion to be reached therefrom would be that the Nicaraguan Constitution of August 19, 1858, is also void. And the reason is because neither the duumvirate which convoked the Assembly, nor the Assembly itself, nor any act done by the one, or the other, did exactly fall under the strict legality of the Constitution of 1838.

Out of the many fundamental laws which the regime aforesaid nullified, one of paramount importance can be cited. This is the same Article 194 of the Constitution of 1838, which the defense of Nicaragua invokes in support of her claim that the treaty of limits is null.

Art. 196 said as follows:

" Art. 196. The present Constitution shall not be revised in its totality until after four years have elapsed, and then, *upon the proper declaration according to the rules of Article 194, that the revision should take place, a Constituent Assembly shall be convoked*, the members of which shall have special and sufficient powers from their constituents."

---

[1] § 262, Chapter xxi, Book I.   [2] I Kent, 162.

But the Constituent Assembly was convoked, and its meetings were held, without the formalities of Art. 194 of the Constitution having been observed at all, either previously or subsequently. If the treaty of limits is null, owing to the non-compliance with that law, the Constitution of 1858, which was framed and promulgated without taking it into consideration, and has the same defect, is also null. Such conclusion would be absurd; but its logical character shows that the Constituent Assembly of 1858 was not bound at all to obey the provisions of the Constitution of 1838, but had authority to act with utmost freedom, so as to obtain the high purposes which the dictatorial duumvirate had called it to accomplish.

In the presence of this doctrine, and of the facts and considerations already set forth, there is not the slightest foundation for the statement that the treaty of 1858 lacks validity because it was made in violation of the fundamental laws of Nicaragua.

Chapter III.

DEMARCATION OF THE TERRITORY OF NICARAGUA ACCORDING TO HER FIRST CONSTITUTION PROMULGATED APRIL 8, 1826—NICOYA.

The present Republic of Nicaragua is nothing else than the old State of the same name organized on the 8th of April, 1826, as one of the members of the Central American Republic.

Chapter 1 of her Constitution, promulgated at the date aforesaid, clearly defines the State and the territory thereof in the following language:

"Article 1st. The State shall retain the name of State of Nicaragua, and it shall consist of all the inhabitants thereof, and form a part of the federation of Central America."

"Article 2d. The territory of the State comprises the Districts of Nicaragua, Granada, Managua, Masaya, Matagalpa, Segovia, Leon, Subtiaba and El Realejo.

" Its limits are: on the east, the Sea of the Antilles; on the north, the State of Honduras; on the west, the Gulf of Conchagua; on the south, the Pacific Ocean, and on the south-east the free State of Costa Rica."

"Article 3d. The above-named territory shall be divided into Departments, the number and limits of which shall be fixed by a special law."

The districts which, at the time of the foundation of the State of Nicaragua, formed it, according to its first Constitution, were Nicaragua, Granada, Managua, Masaya, Matagalpa, Segovia, Leon, Subtiaba, El Realejo, and none else.

The District of Nicoya which, before the independence, had been at different times alternatively attached, sometimes to

[1] *Recopilación de las leyes decretos y acuerdos ejecutivos de la República de Nicaragua en Centro América, formada por el Doctor y Maestro Licenciado Don Jesus de la Rocha, &c., &c.* Managua. Imprenta del Gobierno 1867, page 13.

Nicaragua, sometimes to Costa Rica, and which in the last years of the Spanish rule was united to Costa Rica for some purposes and for other purposes to Nicaragua, but which generally enjoyed a certain degree of independence as a Mayoralty (*Corregimiento*), directly depending upon the crown; the District of Nicoya, which by the sovereign will of its inhabitants had broken, two years before the foundation of the State of Nicaragua, the partial bonds which connected it with that State, and had incorporated itself, with the sanction of the Federal Congress of Central America, into the bordering State of Costa Rica; that district, I say, was not comprised by the first Constitution of Nicaragua in the number of those which formed that State.

So it appears from the plain language of Article 2nd of the organic law of Nicaragua of 1826, which necessarily was the basis upon which the Constitutions of 1838, 1854, 1858, and all others subsequent have been founded.

The exclusion of Nicoya was not only explicit, but unconditional, and without reserve. The Constituent legislators of Nicaragua had before their eyes the accomplished fact, sanctioned by the Federal power, and they respected and recognized it in Article 1st of the Constitution.

This Article is by itself sufficient to leave beyond a doubt that at the time of the organization of the State of Nicaragua, Nicoya did not form a portion of her territory. And the truth of this assertion is confirmed, among many other reasons, by the resolution of May 12, 1830,[1] passed by the Legislative Assembly of Nicaragua, which reads as follows:

" Upon consideration of the motion made by one of the Deputies asking that the District of Nicoya, which AGGREGATED ITSELF TO THE STATE OF COSTA RICA because of the last political convulsions, should be restored to Nicaragua, the legislative body was pleased to resolve: That, whereas, the cause

---

[1] *Recopilación de las leyes decretos y acuerdos ejecutivos de la República de Nicaragua, &c., por el Doctor Don Jesus de la Rocha,* page 66.

4

which brought about that result has ceased to exist, the Executive should urge the Federal Congress to RESTORE THE SAID DISTRICT TO THE CONDITION IN WHICH IT WAS BEFORE; and for this purpose the said Executive is vested with all the authority that may be necessary."

The Nicaraguan Executive, in carrying out the resolution above mentioned, expressed itself in still more precise and conclusive language:

" Let this resolution be complied with," said the Executive, " let it be transmitted to the Supreme Federal Government, and, in doing so, let the Executive of this State explain, that the REINCORPORATION OF THE DISTRICT OF NICOYA into the State of Nicaragua is advisable and necessary; *first*, because the circumstances which gave rise to ITS SEPARATION FROM NICARAGUA AND ITS ANNEXATION TO COSTA RICA have ceased to exist; *second*, because the said REINCORPORATION contributes to the re-establishment of peace, and to the complete reorganization of the State; * * * *fifth*, because Nicoya is indebted to the State of Nicaragua for tithes and other taxes, and the payment of that debt is obstructed by the AGGREGATION OF THAT DISTRICT TO COSTA RICA."

" Let these considerations be urged upon the Supreme Federal Executive, in order that it may be pleased to submit to Congress, with favorable recommendation, if so deemed advisable, THE PETITION OF NICARAGUA FOR THE REINCORPORATION OF NICOYA INTO HER TERRITORY."

The foregoing documents show that in 1830, more than four years after the organization of the State of Nicaragua, the latter was asking the Federal Congress, not through demands or protests, as now alleged, but by humble prayers, for the reincorporation of Nicoya, which was then united to Costa Rica. But the Central American Congress did not deem it advisable to accede to her petition.

That was exactly the state of things when the Constitution of Nicaragua of November 12, 1838, was promulgated.

The desired reincorporation of Nicoya had not taken place;

and evidently the new Constitution could not declare that the sovereignty of Nicaragua extended in the southeast, bordering upon Costa Rica, to a territory much more extensive than that on which it had been established and organized in 1828.

Chapter I of the Constitution of 1838 defines the State and its Territory as follows:

"ARTICLE 1st. The State shall retain the name of State of Nicaragua; it consists of all its inhabitants, and it shall belong, by means of a compact, to the Federation of Central America."

"ARTICLE 2nd. The territory of the State is the same which was before comprised in the Province of Nicaragua; its limits are: on the east and northeast, the State of Honduras; on the west and south, the Pacific Ocean; and on the southeast, the State of Costa Rica. The boundaries with the bordering States shall be marked out by a law which shall be made a part of the Constitution."

ARTICLE 1st plainly establishes the identity of the State, so that the one organized in 1838 and the one constituted in 1826 were one and the same, both having the same territory and both bordering on the southeast with the free State of Costa Rica. That identity was not destroyed by the insertion in Article 2nd of the phrase, "Province of Nicaragua," because in the ancient documents Nicoya and Nicaragua are often mentioned as different provinces, independent of each other; and therefore the expression, "Province of Nicaragua," does not necessarily imply that the District of Nicoya was included.[1]

In the new Constitution, the districts which formed the State were not mentioned. But this omission was cured by the decree of December 2d of the same year, 1838,[2] issued by the same Constituent Assembly, dividing the territory of the State into four departments, namely, east, west, north, and south.

---

[1] See the Report of Bishop Morrell, 1752, pages 24 and 25 of the Argument of Costa Rica.

[2] *Recopilación de leyes*, &c., por el Doctor de la Rocha, p. 401.

Article 15th of the said decree reads as follows:

" THE SOUTHERN DEPARTMENT SHALL COMPRISE NO MORE THAN ONE DISTRICT, NAMED THE RIVAS DISTRICT, UNTIL THE QUESTION BETWEEN THIS GOVERNMENT AND THAT OF COSTA RICA ABOUT THE REINCORPORATION OF THE DISTRICT OF GUANACASTE IS SETTLED."

The Constituent Legislature of Nicaragua of 1838 declared therefore, in the most solemn possible manner, that the Southern Department of the State had only one District (Rivas), and that this had to be so until the question pending with Costa Rica should be settled and THE DISTRICT OF GUANACASTE SHOULD BE REINCORPORATED INTO NICARAGUA.

To reincorporate means in Spanish, according to the Dictionary of the language:[1]

" To incorporate again, to aggregate, or unite, to a political or moral body something which had been separated from it."

If, according to the Decree of December 21, 1838, issued by the Constituent Legislator, the District of Guanacaste could not be counted among the districts of the southern Department until it was reincorporated into Nicaragua, there is no doubt that the Constitution of 1838 did not declare, nor could it do so, that Guanacaste was an integral part of the Nicaraguan territory. The reincorporation may have been strongly desired ; but it was not accomplished.

The truth is, indeed, that the question pending between Costa Rica and Nicaragua upon this subject did not reach a settlement until the treaty of 1858 was made ; and by it Costa Rica ceded to Nicaragua not only a portion of Guanacaste, but also a portion of the Costa Rican territory which had never belonged to the ancient District of Nicoya. Those ceded territories became Nicaraguan on and after the date of

---

[1] *Diccionario de la lengua Castellana por la Academia española.* Madrid, 1884. Imprenta de Don Gregorio Hernandez.

The same definition is given by Webster (An American Dictionary of the English Language, 1881), by Worcester (A Dictionary of the English Language, Boston, 1860), by Larousse (Grand Dictionnaire Universel du XIX siècle, Paris, 1875) and by Calvo (Dictionnaire de Droit International Public et Privé, Paris, 1885).

the treaty, but the rest of the Costa Rican territory, Guanacaste included, remained as foreign to Nicaragua as it had been prior to the foundation of the two States.

After the Nicaraguan Constitution of 1826 eliminated, unconditionally and without reserve, from the Nicaraguan territory the District of Nicoya, and after the bond which formerly had united it to Nicaragua was thereby severed, all declarations made in subsequent Constitutions, no matter how express, in regard to sovereignty over Nicoya, if ever made, which I deny upon the evidence above given, can have no other character than that of mere *claims* or *pretensions*, as far distant from truth and perfect right, as simple thoughts or wishes are from actual reality.

As the fortune of a merchant is not increased because he records in his books future and eventual profits, likewise the dominions of a sovereign are not enlarged because he writes on a Constitution the names of provinces not actually subject to his rule.

And what cannot be obtained by means of express and known declarations, which may, in time, be refuted and blotted out, much less can be obtained by mystic phrases of hidden meaning, written a long time ago, when no one dreamt that such a construction could be ever placed on them.

To suppose under this singular course of reasoning, that Nicoya was an integral part of Nicaragua is to ignore the fact that, during more than half a century after the Independence and organization of the Central American States, that District, actually and legally was separated from Nicaragua and incorporated into Costa Rica, and that, during the whole of that period, it kept so separated, and formed a part of one of the five provinces of Costa Rica, with whom it has identified itself absolutely in interests, customs, and institutions, to such an extent that citizens of Nicoya have exercised the supreme power, the command of the Army, the Presidency of the National Congress, and filled the positions of Secretary of State, Diplomatic Ministers, Justices of the Supreme Court, &c., &c.

In the face of these facts the pretension ceases to be absurd, and becomes one which, in reality, can be impeached as lacking seriousness.

Nicaragua reasons about Guanacaste, as if she were dealing with things and not with persons; and forgets that the people of that Department, in the exercise of an imprescriptible right, decided to separate, and actually separated, themselves from the Nicaraguan nation, even before said nation was organized as a free State, that the segregation was sanctioned by the common sovereign, which was the Federal Central American power, and that to complete the transaction Nicaragua herself recognized, accepted, and proclaimed it solemnly in its first Constitution. Neither the Constitution of 1838 nor that of 1854, nor any other ever promulgated in Nicaragua, did declare at any time a square inch of territory beyond the limit assigned to the State by the Constitution of 1826 to be Nicaraguan domain. Nor could any Constitution have done so except in case that the territorial acquisition would have been made after 1826, which never happened except under the treaty of 1858, which gave Nicaragua a portion of Guanacaste.

There is not, therefore, as far as Guanacaste is concerned, the slightest conflict between the treaty of 1858 and the Constitution of Nicaragua; and to maintain the contrary is completely to lose sight of the public law of that country and of the rudiments of its history, or of the Constitution of April 8, 1826, which was the first one ever promulgated in Nicaragua, and under which she presented herself as a free Central American State in the community of nations.

Better informed than the public men of Nicaragua seems to have been the Minister of the United States in that country, Mr. Charles N. Riotte, who, in his despatch to the Secretary of State, Mr. Fish, dated at Managua on June 20, 1872, says the following:

" It is a matter of history that since 1824, WITHOUT INTERRUPTION, the Province of Guanacaste formed an integral part of the Republic of Costa Rica. Nothing has more embittered the feeling in Costa Rica than this eternal harping for the 'lost brethren' by the Nicaraguans, keeping up in the minds of the inhabitants of that Province an insecurity and uneasiness, the principal cause of its miserable condition. It is really too bad that these people, barely able to exercise its authority on one-third of its undisputed territory, and incapable of making it felt over two-thirds thereof, should run riot after a distant, wretched province, separated from the bulk of the Republic by high mountain ranges, inaccessible for six months in the year, and heedlessly provoke the enmity of a comparatively powerful neighbor."[1]

And as the District of Nicoya or Guanacaste was not, according to the declarations of the Nicaraguan Constitutions of 1826 and 1838, an integral part of the State of Nicaragua, as has been proved above, it is a grave error to maintain that the treaty of 1858 amended the Constitution of Nicaragua, and that it has no value because the amendment made by it was not in accordance with the forms and solemnities prescribed for such cases by the Constitution of that State.

[1] Papers relating to the Foreign Relations of the United States in 1873, page 738.

Chapter IV.

DEMARCATION OF THE TERRITORY OF NICARAGUA ACCORDING TO ITS FIRST CONSTITUTION—SOUTHERN BANK OF THE SAN JUAN RIVER.

BESIDES the claim that her sovereignty extends according to her Constitution of 1838 to the territory of Guanacaste, Nicaragua set forth that she is entitled under the same Constitution to all the land adjoining the San Juan river down to the mouth of the Colorado river.

It is easy to show that that pretension is groundless.

If the text of the Constitution of Nicaragua of 1826, which has been copied in the preceding chapter is examined, it will be found that not a word exists in that instrument in support of the idea that the southern bank of the San Juan river was Nicaraguan territory, but, on the contrary, it will appear that the Constitution declares the territory of the State to border on that side upon the free State of Costa Rica.

This State had organized itself on January 21, 1825, under a constitution, which was communicated to the Federal Powers, in which it is said that the Costa Rican territory on the side of the Northern Sea ended at the mouth of the San Juan river. Therefore the Constitution of Nicaragua, which was subsequent, far from supporting the idea now set forth by her Government, rather establishes the truth of the contrary assertion, because it was in the power of Nicaragua to contradict the declaration made by the Costa Rican organic law, and she not only failed to do so, but fixed as a limit of Nicaragua the same one which the free State of Costa Rica, organized a little more than one year before, had designated.

The state of things in Nicaragua in 1838 being the same as in 1826, the Constitution promulgated on the former date could not enlarge the territory of the State and carry the frontier beyond the San Juan river.

But even supposing that such a thing happened, which never did, such a declaration, in conflict with the first Costa Rican Constitution which had been accepted and recognized, never could prevail against it; and the result would be that the Nicaraguan declaration was of no more value than a simple claim or pretension, made still less meritorious by the fact that Costa Rica found herself in actual and immemorial possession of the territory, and Nicaragua never possessed it, nor exercised over it any act of domain.

In the first part of this reply the possession of Costa Rica of the southern bank of the San Juan river, before the Independence and since, up to the date of the treaty, in which her rights of bordering nation were somewhat restricted, has been proved.

All the legislative collections of Nicaragua since the 10th of April, 1825, in which her first Constituent Congress met, can be perused, and no act will be found which supports or authorizes the claim that she exercised sovereign rights over the zone above mentioned.

Political constitutions, on the other hand, are not the places where questions of limits between the States are to be defined. Otherwise such questions would never be settled without a general upsetting of the State being caused by the variation of its organic law.

Almost every country, especially in America, has had questions of territorial limits with its neighbors, and they have been settled by public treaties, which had never been given the character of constitutional amendments. And this being the case, all the said treaties, without exception, could be held void, as made in violation of the respective national Constitutions.

This irremedial nullity would be incurred, among many others, by the treaty by which Louisiana was ceded to the United States; by the treaty of Guadalupe-Hidalgo, by which Mexico renounced her sovereignty over the territories of Upper California, Colorado, Nevada, and New Mexico; by the treaty between Spain and France of 1856, which settled a question of limits standing for centuries; by the treaty between France and Italy, by which Savoy and Nice were annexed to France, to the detriment of Italy; by the treaty of 1866, by which Chili ceded to Bolivia a portion of the Atacama Desert; by the treaty of 1876, by which the Argentine Republic ceded a portion of territory to that of Paraguay; by the treaty of 1883, by which the annexation of Chiapas and Soconusco to Mexico was finally recognized, &c., &c.

No one of these treaties has ever been considered as an amendment to the Constitutions of the countries which entered into them. And if the course of reasoning of Nicaragua is accepted, the conclusion cannot be avoided that they all are invalid. A doctrine which leads to such conclusions needs not to be refuted. To show its logical consequences is sufficient to reject it.

Chapter V.

ONE of the erroneous ideas on which the argument of Nicaragua rests, consists in considering the compact of 1858, not as a public international convention like any other, but as an amendment to, or a reform of, the Nicaraguan Constitution.

It has been already shown, in Chapters III and IV, how groundless this assertion is in matter of fact, since the Constitutions of Nicaragua could not comprise, nor did they comprise under her sovereignty, the territory of Nicoya, now Province of Guanacaste, and much less the lands adjoining the San Juan river on its southern bank.

Now I shall proceed to show the incorrectness of the same idea from another standpoint.

By means of conjectures and interpretations, more or less strained, Nicaragua tries to persuade that the treaty of limits modified or amended Article 2d of the Constitution of 1838. But this pretension has been beforehand rejected and refuted by Nicaragua herself, through the organ of her Constituent Assembly of 1858, which by positive and express action, admitting of no contradiction, declared and proclaimed the contrary.

If, as it is claimed, the treaty of limits would have involved or implied, in the mind of the Constituent Legislator of Nicaragua, a constitutional reform or amendment, no doubt can be entertained, that for concluding and perfecting it the Constituent Assembly would have proceeded in the same way, as it did, for the special constitutional amendments which it decreed, in all of which it took pains to express by a final article the constituent or organic character of its action.

If this was not done, if the Constituent Assembly did not

subject the treaty to the rules of proceedings and to the forms which correspond to a constitutional amendment, if no one said, or thought, at that time, that the treaty implied such an amendment, it is plain, as well as indisputable, that the Assembly did not give the treaty a different character than that which belongs to any other public treaties whatsoever; and this opinion of the Assembly, certainly one in conformity with truth and principle, this authentic interpretation made by the Nicaraguan Constituent Legislator himself, is the most eloquent negative answer that can be given to the allegations of the latter Governments of Nicaragua which attempt to attribute to the treaty of limits a character which does not belong to it.

If the Constituent Assembly of 1858 would have had in its mind that when approving the treaty it was merely approving it for the first time, subject to the action of a subsequent legislature, which might sanction or reject it, it would not have eliminated from the law of territorial division of the Republic which it enacted on August 30, 1858,[1] the reservation clause in regard to Guanacaste, which the Constituent Assembly of 1838 had written in its own law of territorial division of December 21st of that year.[2] It is plain that if such had been the case the Constituent Assembly would have postponed the elimination until the moment in which the subsequent legislature should give its approval.

But no such thing happened, and the new territorial division was made by law as follows:

"ARTICLE 1. The Republic is divided for electoral purposes into seven departments, to wit: Chinandega, Leon, Nueva Segovia, Matagalpa, Chontales, Rivas, and Granada."

*   *   *   *   *   *   *

"ARTICLE 8. The District of Rivas (bordering with Guanacaste) consists of the city of this name, the town of San Jorge,

See Gaceta de Nicaragua, No. 39, Nov. 20, 1856.
[2] Recopilacion de las leyes &c. de Nicaragua, por el Dr. La Rocha, Managua, 1867, page 401

Buenos Ayres, Potosí, Obrage, Ometepe, Moyagalpa, Pineda, La Virgen, and Tortugal."

No reservation of any kind is made here in regard to Guanacaste or Nicoya, because the question which had been pending between the two Republics about that territory was then finally settled by the treaty of limits.

The Constituent Assembly of 1858 gave to the treaty its true character, and all the Executives and all the Legislatures subsequent to that year, up to 1871, always agreed in regard to this point. Nothing will be found, whether in the statute books of Nicaragua, nor in the action of her administration, nor in the decrees of the Nicaraguan courts from 1858 to 1871, which involves the idea that the treaty of limits was an imperfect and unfinished amendment to the Constitution of the country ; while, on the contrary, the proofs are abundant that the said treaty was always recognized and considered, not as something incomplete and still pending, but as a convention finally concluded and sanctioned.

The reasons now alleged to give to the convention of limits of 1858 no more character than that of a projected constitutional reform never consummated, must be exceedingly weak when they never occurred to the mind of any of the Supreme Powers of Nicaragua from 1858 to 1871. They must be very weak, indeed, when they were never used before the downfall of the Ayón-Chevalier contract, or under the eventful circumstances of 1864, when Nicaragua suspended her relations with Costa Rica, because of the hospitality which, according to her laws, she could not refuse, and which she extended to the ex-President of Salvador, General Don Gerardo Barrios.

CHAPTER VI.

EVEN GRANTING THAT THE TREATY OF 1858 INVOLVED A CESSION OF TERRI-
TORY, THIS CESSION COULD BE MADE BY ONLY ONE LEGISLATURE ACCORD-
ING TO THE CONSTITUTION OF 1838.

IF the Constitutions of Nicaragua prior to 1858 are con-
sulted nothing will be found in them clearly and directly explaining which are the authorities or officers of the State, in
whom the power of validly contracting in the name of the
nation is vested. For this reason it is necessary for us to turn
to the general principles which in countries under democratic
institutions vest that power jointly in the Chief Magistrate
of the State and the national representation.

But the national representation and the supreme Chief
Magistrate of Nicaragua were precisely the ones who made
the treaty of 1858 ; and, therefore, the conclusion cannot be
avoided that the treaty is valid and perfect under the most
strict principles of international law.

Perhaps the very circumstance that the Constitution of 1838
was so silent in regard to the treaty-making power induced the
Constituent Assembly to enact special laws for the conclusion,
ratification, and exchange of the treaty of limits of 1858.
That treaty was not, as it is supposed, the work of the Executive, simply approved but not sanctioned by the Constituent
Assembly, but a legislative act, perfected and consummated, in
which the Executive acted not only in its capacity as such, but
as delegate of the Constituent Assembly, under instructions
and upon bases furnished by the said Assembly, to which it
strictly adhered.

It is claimed in the argument of Nicaragua that the treaty of
1858 involved a cession or alienation of the national territory,
and that, under this circumstance, which dismembered the
State, the treaty could have no value without the requisites
prescribed for constitutional amendments being first complied
with.

There is error in believing that the treaty had the effect of transferring to Costa Rica a portion of the territory of Nicaragua. This has already been proved. But, even supposing that such a transfer was made, the treaty would, nevertheless, be valid, because the Nicaraguan Legislative Power, according to Article 109 of the Constitution of 1838, had authority to alienate the national territory without needing for that purpose to amend the Constitution. And if a simple, ordinary legislature had that power, the Constituent Assembly of 1858, which represented the nation without any of the limitations of an ordinary Congress, must also have had it with still more reason.

See what the above-said Article 109 of the Constitution of 1838 says in this respect:

"It belongs to the legislative power of the State—

"1st. To enact, interpret, and abrogate the laws when necessary.

"9th. To resolve what may be advisable about the administration, preservation, and ALIENATION OF ALL PROPERTY OF THE STATE."

The defense of Costa Rica tries to disguise as much as it can the constituent character of the Assembly of 1858 which approved the treaty; but, even supposing that it had been a mere ordinary Congress, or Legislature, bound to act necessarily within the limits of the Constitution of 1838, and also that the treaty involved an alienation of State property, that ordinary Congress had, however, full power to give its approval to the treaty without transgressing the Constitutional rules.

It is well, therefore, for Vattel to say that the Chief of the State cannot alienate its territory, and that the nation itself must do it. This principle was precisely the one which was applied to the present case. The nation itself, by means of a Constituent Assembly, approved the treaty, and nothing else can be demanded.

Chapter VII.

THE title of this chapter indicates the assertion of one of the three reasons given by the representative of Nicaragua in support of the claim that the treaty of 1858 is null and void.

It is alleged that, under Article XII of that instrument, it had to be ratified, and the ratifications exchanged within forty days after its conclusion; that the exchange was made on April 26th of the same year by the Presidents of Costa Rica and Nicaragua, before the treaty was approved by the Assembly; that the treaty was approved, not ratified, on June 4 subsequent, when thirty-eight days had already elapsed since the date of the exchange; and, lastly, that the day on which the Assembly gave its approval, the period of 40 days fixed by the treaty for the exchange had expired.

This new argument of Nicaragua is as weak and untenable as all others set forth by her.

It would be necessary that neither the Presidents of Costa Rica and Nicaragua, nor their respective Cabinets, nor the Chambers of either Republic, nor, in one word, any person whatsoever in the two countries, knew at the time of the celebration of the treaty the meaning of the word ratification used therein, nor the importance and transcendency of the act expressed by it, nor its indispensable priority to the exchange, to suppose that, notwithstanding the express provision of the treaty, they decided to make the exchange without a previous ratification, and without being fully persuaded that the form in which the said ratification had been imparted was sufficient and valid.

It can never be admitted that serious men could have compromised in such an inconsiderate way the acts of two Governments, and the transcendency of a compact of such importance as the one fixing the limits between the two countries, . purporting to be a settlement of protracted questions, and a happy termination of an unpleasant state of things, which, consequently, was received by the people of both countries with signs of jubilation, more so, perhaps, by Nicaragua herself, who went so far as to confer the rank of a general in her army on the Salvadorian mediator.

According to the decree, to be found elsewhere in this reply, the Constituent Assembly of Nicaragua, in use of the full power vested in it, *delegated* to the Chief Magistrate of the nation for the sake of brevity, and owing to the importance of the matter, the faculty to ratify the treaty, provided that it was in accordance with the bases that had been communicated to him for his guidance.

In this there was no irregularity of any kind, because the people themselves, by means of their representatives entrusted with framing the organic law, had a perfect right to delegate their faculties to whomsoever they pleased ; and there was no harm either, whatever the gravity of the subject might have been, because, as long as the act was performed in strict accordance with the instructions and bases given by the Assembly, the Assembly itself was in reality the party which concluded the treaty, and the ratification became unnecessary, or, better to say, it was given beforehand.

That the treaty of limits of 1858 did not go a single point beyond the instructions given by the Assembly is clearly proved by the fact of the approval which that body imparted to it, and furthermore by the unanimous and warm acceptance which it received by the public press of Nicaragua and by the whole nation, as well as by the immediate execution of its provisions and its enforcement during a long period of time.

The very fact of the approval of the treaty by the Assembly, which is invoked as an argument in support of the alleged want of ratification, proves *a posteriori* that that body considered both the treaty and the exchange, in the form in which they were made, and the time thereof, as perfectly valid acts ;

5

because, otherwise, if the Assembly had thought that the requisite of ratification was wanting, it either would have ratified it, if so deemed advisable, or would have withheld its sanction expressly, whether on the ground that the treaty did not suit its ideas, or because the forty days agreed upon fory the ratification or exchange had elapsed. Therefore if the Assembly, with full knowledge of the manner in which the treaty was celebrated and of the way and date in which the exchange was made, and of the fact that the period agreed upon for the ratification had passed, approved the treaty, it is evident that it judged, as was the truth, that the treaty had been legally and in due time ratified by the President, in use of the special faculties which had been vested in him for that purpose.

To think otherwise would be equivalent to saying that the most eminent men of Nicaragua, who formed the Constituent Assembly of 1858, were incapable of seeing such palpable defects as those which are now alleged, and that that incapacity was carried to the extreme, because it was exhibited in regard to acts of their own, just publicly accomplished.

The very same words of President Martinez and the Assembly in regard to the treaty clearly show what their intention was, and what was the especial course which, according to the abnormal condition of the Republic and the peculiar character of the subject, they had intended to pursue. Those words also show that they had a clear insight into what they were doing. The President, contrary to the general custom, because the Executive, as a general rule, confines its action only to the *approval* of the treaties, *ratified* the one of 1858; and the Assembly, differently, also, from the usual custom of those bodies which are called to RATIFY the international Convention, confined itself TO APPROVE the one herein referred to.

The President ratified, because he had delegated authority to do so; and the Assembly approved, because what is already ratified needs no further ratification.

The treaty of 1858 was, therefore, ratified by the one who had full authority to do so, and the ratification, as well as the exchange, took place within the stipulated time. With this the remark made by the representative of Nicaragua as to the want of exchange of the treaty, after its approval by the Assembly, has been answered.

This fact, which is correct, corroborates the efficiency which Costa Rica, as well as Nicaragua, gave, both at the time of the conclusion of the treaty, and during fourteen years of uninterrupted compliance with it, to the ratification made by the President and to the exchange which followed it. Costa Rica never thought of asking for any exchange of the treaty after the approval by the Assembly, because none was to be made. The exchange had already been made within the period fixed by the treaty, and not only with all the required solemnity, but with luxury of forms, as I have explained elsewhere.

CHAPTER VIII

WHETHER THE TREATY OF 1858 WAS RATHER IMPOSED UPON NICARAGUA THAN ACCEPTED BY HER.

IN the preceding argument of Costa Rica, Chapter XI of the Second Part, the true history of the negotiations which culminated in the convention of limits of April 15, 1858, was given with minute correctness, supported by documents. It would, therefore, be idle for Costa Rica to say here anything further in regard to that point, if she were not compelled to rectify certain assertions made in the Argument of Nicaragua, which are absolutely at variance with truth.

The said Argument set forth affirmatively that Costa Rica, in flagrant violation of international law, without a previous declaration of war, and with the animus of taking possession by force of a portion of the Nicaraguan territory, which all her diplomatic efforts had not been able to secure, profiting by the state of prostration in which Nicaragua was at that time, invaded her territory and occupied the San Juan river, which gave occasion to the intervention of Salvador, and to the treaty of 1858 "imposed upon Nicaragua rather than accepted by her."

It is a fact of indisputable notoriety that one and all of the propositions which I have just transcribed are in opposition to historical truth.

Costa Rica and the other States of Central America, except Nicaragua, enjoyed in 1856 the benefits of peace; but the civil struggles between Granadines and Leonese furnished occasion and reason for the war which Costa Rica, Guatemala, Honduras, and Salvador were compelled, in spite of themselves, in union with a portion of the people of Nicaragua, to wage against General William Walker, the usurper of the public power in the latter country.

All the allied nations remained more or less prostrated on account of that war, and none certainly more so than Costa Rica and Nicaragua, which bore the greatest part of its burden.

The differences concerning territorial limits were absolutely forgotten under those circumstances of common danger for all Central America. And if Costa Rica carried her forces to Nicaragua, as she certainly did, it was not as an invader or enemy, but as a friend and ally; and if she took possession of Walker's steamers and with them ruled over the San Juan river and the Lake, she did so with the approval and consent of the Nicaraguan party which struggled for the independence of their country, and in pursuance of a treaty of alliance, offensive and defensive, with all the other States of Central America, solemnly promulgated and approved and applauded, not only by every good Nicaraguan and the whole Central American people, but by other nations whose safety had been indirectly threatened.

The only protest which, under those circumstances, was raised against Costa Rica, was on the part of Walker and his followers. But he, in Nicaragua, was only an usurper, both hateful and tyrannical.

The seizure of the steamers and the control of the river and the Lake is one of the greatest sources of pride and national glory for Costa Rica. That exploit was the severest blow ever inflicted upon the growing power of Walker, as he himself acknowledged in his history of the Nicaraguan war. The documents and publications of that time all agree in considering those facts as decisive of the final victory.

It is therefore scarcely conceivable that this being the case the name of flagrant violation of international law should be given to the most signal act of assistance and friendship which Nicaragua could receive under those circumstances.

To co-operate as an ally, to redeem a sister nation from the foreign yoke to which she had been subjected, and which she after a severe struggle had proved to be powerless to shake off, is not to violate international law, but, on the contrary, fulfill perhaps excessively, the duty of reciprocal assistance which sister nations like those of Central America owe to each other.

Costa Rica retained during the war the positions which she had gained by her effort, in order that they would not fall again into the hands of the enemy to the prejudice of all the allies. But Nicaragua, as soon as she saw the prominence which her neighbor had reached became jealous and diffident, and in the moment, which certainly was the least opportune, took up the forgtoten question of limits.

This action gave occasion to unpleasantness which might have led to war, if the prudence of Costa Rica had not avoided it.

Finally, owing in great part to the efforts of Salvador, all the differences were compromised and adjusted by the treaty of 1858, which was initiated, negotiated, ratified, exchanged, promulgated, and enforced after Nicaragua was in full, quiet, and peaceful possession of her waters, her territory, her fortresses, her ports, and her cities and towns, and when she was at the most perfect peace, cordiality, and harmony with Costa Rica.

To say, therefore, that the treaty of 1858, rather than accepted by Nicaragua, was imposed upon her by Costa Rica, is asserting a fact not only absolutely at variance with truth, but offensive to Nicaragua, who is supposed thereby to be capable of signing an unacceptable treaty, for fear of incurring the anger of her neighbor.

Such conclusions are reached when a cause is defended with arguments not resting upon truth.

CHAPTER IX.

WHETHER THE TREATY OF LIMITS IS NULL FOR WANT OF RATIFICATION BY THE GOVERNMENT OF SALVADOR.

IN Chapters X, XII, XIII, and XIV of the Second Part of the preceding Argument of Costa Rica, the questions arising out of the want of ratification of the treaty of 1858 by the Republic of Salvador were fully considered, and it was shown therein that that want of ratification does not affect in any way or manner the validity of the compact as to the principal contracting parties.

The reasons which the defense of Nicaragua alleges in the Argument to which I reply have been already amply refuted in the Argument of Costa Rica; and, indeed, there is not a single passage in the Nicaraguan Argument which needs now to be answered.

The whole reasoning of Nicaragua upon this subject can be summed up in the following propositions :

A.—The guarantee of Salvador was a stipulation introduced into the treaty to the exclusive benefit of Nicaragua and against Costa Rica.

But this proposition cannot be maintained in the presence of Article IX of the same treaty, which reads as follows :

" Under no circumstances, and even in case that the Republics of Costa Rica and Nicaragua should unhappily find themselves in a state of war, neither of them shall be allowed to commit any act of hostility against the other, whether in the port of San Juan del Norte or in the San Juan river or the Lake of Nicaragua."

As it is seen, the stipulation is mutual, and introduced for the benefit of both countries, and equally restraining upon them—not by any means a right for one, and a charge upon the other, as Nicaragua pretends.

B.—The guarantee of Salvador was the principal consideration which induced Nicaragua to assent to the treaty.

Should this be true, Nicaragua would not have shown quite as much anxiety as Costa Rica for settling the question of limits which, for more than thirty years, had kept the two countries in a constant state of uneasiness. Neither would she have shown so much interest in acquiring peacefully, and in a manner not subject to contradiction, the southern shore of the Great Lake, and a portion of the right bank of the San Juan river, as well as the portion of territory which the treaty gave her south of the Sapoá and La Flor rivers,—or in securing the perpetual alliance of Costa Rica for the defense of the San Juan river and the port of San Juan, and acquiring the eminent domain and sovereignty over the waters of the San Juan river, in which she only had, up to that time, the right of possession in common,—or in releasing herself from the payment of the considerable amount of money which she owed to Costa Rica. Nothing of this would have happened if the treaty had been intended merely to secure for Nicaragua the important right of not being harassed by hostilities by her neighbor on the waters of the San Juan river and the other places designated. See, therefore, how far from being correct is the proposition under consideration.

C.—The treaty of limits was a tripartite convention, and cannot have either value or effect without the unanimous consent of all the parties who subscribed to it.

The inexactness of this proposition is self evident, when it is considered, as has been superabundantly proved, that the Government of Salvador was not an essential party to the treaty of limits between Costa Rica and Nicaragua, but that it was primarily a friendly mediator and subsequently a secondary party, as surety or guarantor, a character which could disappear without affecting in the least the principal obligation.

D.—If the consent of all the parties is wanting, and one of the stipulations of the treaty falls thereby, the whole treaty must also fall, because " any special advantage conceded by a party under any one article of the compact is in consideration of all the advantages enjoyed by the same party under that and all other articles of the treaty.

To support this conclusion a passage of an opinion of Mr. Cushing, Attorney-General of the United States, has been quoted.

If Nicaragua pretends by this argument that the guarantee in favor of the stipulation of Article X of the treaty offered by the Minister of Salvador in the name of his Government is one of those special advantages conceded to one party by the other in exchange and in compensation of all the other advantages that the granting party enjoys under the whole compact, the structure of her argument proves to be faulty.

The guarantee spoken of was not a special advantage for Nicaragua, nor was it conceded by Costa Rica, but it was, as plainly expressed by the language of the Article, a mutual advantage stipulated in favor of the two contracting nations without difference or preference of any kind between them, and in consideration of nothing else than a mere general Central American interest felt by a third party, which was the Government of Salvador.

So that, even following the course of reasoning of the defense of Nicaragua in regard to this point, and even admitting, what cannot be admitted without doing extreme violence to the doctrine of contracts, that the promise or guarantee without sufficient consideration was not a simple *nudus pactus*, having no more value than that of the paper upon which it was written, the result would always be that the said doctrine has no application in this case.

If the party who "conceded," or offered to concede, that "advantage" had been Costa Rica, the application of the doctrine might take place, because, in that case, the advantage, whether special or not, conceded by her might be claimed to be in consideration of all the other advantages which the whole of the treaty secured for her. But, as the alleged "advantage" is nothing which one of the parties offered to the other, but something that was offered to the two equally and at the same time by a third party, who acted as a mediator, it is plain that it could not form part of the consideration of the treaty. The advantage was not granted by Costa Rica, and, therefore, it cannot be understood to be a consideration for the "advantages" which the whole treaty stipulated in her favor.

The opponent has tried to dazzle the upright and impartial criterion of the Arbitrator by referring to a passage, both incomplete and inapplicable, of an opinion of Mr. Cushing.

True it is that on October 14, 1853, that distinguished jurist was called upon by the Secretary of State of the United States, Mr. Marcy, to give his opinion upon a certain pretension of the Chargé d'Affaires of Denmark in this country, to the effect that certain seamen who had deserted a Danish vessel should be surrendered to him on the ground that the United States, by treaty with the Government of Sweden, had bound themselves to do so when the deserting seamen were Swedish, and that Denmark under the clause "of most favored nation," stipulated in the treaty celebrated with her, was entitled to enjoy the same advantage.

Mr. Cushing maintained that if the grant made in favor of Sweden had been gratuitous, Denmark might have the right, under her own treaty, to share like benefits. But that, whereas the "advantage" conceded to Sweden was something intimately connected with all the other "advantages" granted by her, it was not possible to extend it to Denmark under the clause "of most favored nation," unless under circumstances entirely identical and upon Denmark's giving the entirety of the compensation granted by Sweden.[1]

It is, therefore, plain that the defense of Nicaragua, picking up detached phrases of a respectable text, distorts its meaning.

And the proof thereof is that Mr. Cushing himself, in the same opinion and a few lines below the passage quoted by the

---

[1] Opinions of the Attorneys-General of the United States, vol. vi, page 148.

opponent, says that " neither party to a treaty can, of its mere will and pleasure, abrogate such agreement, except under agreed conditions;" and that "the league, *ligamen*, can be rightfully dissolved only by the same mutuality of consent by which it was tied," which being brought and applied to the present case teaches Nicaragua that the treaty which she made with Costa Rica, giving away certain things and receiving others in exchange, cannot be rescinded, for the mere reason that such agreement, for some cause or other, does not now suit her convenience; and that on the contrary she has to admit it as valid and efficient as she has willingly done for many years.

CHAPTER X

ONE of the arguments of the learned opponent in favor of the nullity of the treaty consists in the allegation that Nicaragua was injured by it.

"It is laid down by Vattel," says the Argument of Nicaragua, "that a treaty pernicious to the State is null, and not at all obligatory, as no conductor of a nation has the power to enter into engagements to do such things as are capable of destroying the State, for whose safety the Government is entrusted to him;" and in further proof of this assertion, the same argument refers to the precedent of the treaty of Madrid of 1526 between Emperor Charles V and the King of France, Francis I; and also the renunciation of Maria Theresa. From here it concludes that the treaty which fixed the territorial limits of the two nations twenty-nine years ago must be consigned to oblivion, and stricken from the Statute Books of Nicaragua.

The first thing to be said in answer to this argument is that neither the quotation from Vattel is complete, nor is the case referred to by that illustrious author in the passage quoted the same as the treaty of Nicaragua. In the same place, in which Vattel explains what, in his judgment, must be done with pernicious treaties, that is in § 160 of Chapter XII, Book II, of his standard work on the "Law of Nations," he recommends the reader to turn his eyes to some other portion of his work, and consider what he himself had said in former paragraphs of the same Chapter and Book, and also in Chapter XXI of the preceding Book I.

There Vattel says as follows:

"A treaty is valid when there is no vice in the manner in

which it was concluded, and for this *nothing else can be demanded* than a sufficient power in the contracting parties and their mutual consent sufficiently declared." [1]

The same distinguished writer says in continuation as follows: "*The hardship (lessio) cannot make a treaty invalid.*" The one who enters into a contract must look well on what he does and weigh with care everything before giving his consent. He can do whatever he pleases with what is his; he can waive his rights or give up his advantages, and the other party, although benefitted by his action, has no obligation to inquire into the reasons which moved him to act, or to weigh the just value of his acts. *If a treaty could be repudiated because one of the parties to it deems itself wronged there would be nothing lasting in* the contracts among nations."

"The happiness and peace of the nations manifestly demand that their treaties should not depend upon a cause of nullity so vague and dangerous." [2]

We are taught upon the authority of the same great writer that those treaties which settle by means of a compromise differences among nations, although necessarily implying losses and renunciations, sometimes of considerable importance, are not only valid but highly commendable. [3]

"It is commonly laid down," says Bernard, "that neither the plea of 'duress,' nor that of *lessio enormis* (a degree of hardship that is so plain and gross that the sufferer cannot be supposed to have contemplated what he was undertaking) recognized directly or circuitously, in one form or another, by municipal law, both ancient and modern, can be allowed to justify the non-fulfilment of a treaty." [4]

But even in case that the treaty of limits which Nicaragua signed, ratified, and promulgated in 1858, subjected her to losses, and really did injury, is it not plain that such injury

---

[1] § 141, Chapter xii, Book ii.
[2] § 158, Chapter ii, Book ii.
[3] § 329, Chapter xviii, Book ii.
[4] Bernard on Diplomacy, 85.
Dr. Wharton's Digest, Chapter vi, § 132, Vol. ii, p. 5.

cannot be other than that naturally involved in all compromises ?

Such a commendable manner of putting an end to litigation, as a compromise is, implies by its own essence on the part of both contracting parties the sacrifice of some rights, no matter how well founded, and thus excludes at once all idea that it is possible to rescind it on account of hardship.

If an injury of that kind is alleged by Nicaragua for the purpose of causing the treaty of 1858 to fall, with how much more reason could Costa Rica allege it ? She lost by the treaty the eminent domain on the San Juan river, and her condition and rights as a riparian State for an extent equal to the third part of the course of the river and the whole of the southern part of the Lake ; and, furthermore, she lost a considerable zone of territory on the Papagallo Isthmus from the La Flor river to the centre of the Salinas Bay.

The above stated doctrine, held by the laws of all civilized nations to be correct, is obvious ; and there is no writer on International Law who contradicts it.

CHAPTER XI

THERE is a point extensively treated in the Argument of Costa Rica, upon which not a word would be added in the present reply, if Nicaragua had not boasted in her Argument of the firmness with which for many continuous years she has maintained the invalidity of the treaty of 1858.

In contrast with the persistence with which it is true that Nicaragua has maintained, subsequent to 1872, the above said idea, I shall present now some facts not set forth in my former Argument, which testify to the respect which that treaty received in Nicaragua prior to that year.

The preliminary arrangement Volio-Zelaya, signed in San José on July 13, 1868,[1] shows that on that date the Government of Nicaragua recognized the force of the treaty of limits. Otherwise the said Government would not have tried to secure the acquiescence of the Government of Costa Rica for the improvement of the San Juan river and of the Bay of San Juan del Norte which was then in project.

Another fact is the following:

The official newspaper of Nicaragua, in commenting upon the speech of Licentiate Don Jesus Jimenez, President of Costa Rica, in the official reception of Señor Don Mariano Montealegre, Envoy Extraordinary and Minister Plenipotentiary of Nicaragua, expressed itself in the following remarkable language:

" *But Nicaragua and Costa Rica find themselves in condition on account of their topographic position, if it is so desired, to strengthen still more these bonds, and work with greater*

---

[1] See Document No. 53.

effort in uniting their interests for the sake of human progress."

" The San Juan river, while dividing the two States territorially, mixes in such a way in its bountiful waters the commercial interests of both nations, as not to allow either one to be indifferent to anything happening on it."

This was written on May 22, 1869, and it shows that at that date it was still in the mind of Nicaragua that the stipulations of the treaty of 1858 were binding upon her.

A few days afterwards civil war came again to afflict that country. Among the instructions which, with supreme approval, were given to the Military Inspector of the Lake and San Juan river, the following appears:

" The line of the San Juan river is one of the most important positions which the Government needs to retain. The efforts of the revolution may be made on that side. * * * To strike a blow upon that line is, therefore, the best thing to be done, because they (the enemies) may attempt *to take possession of the frontier of Costa Rica* to make of it the bases of their operations."

" It may also happen that the Government of Costa Rica, alarmed by the revolution of Nicaragua, * * * acting with exaggerated zeal, and possibly trusting in the inability of the Government of this Republic TO PROTECT THE POINTS ON THIS LINE, may attempt to take possession of El Castillo and of the San Cárlos fortresses for the purpose of protecting itself (the Government of Costa Rica) against any attempt of INVASION OF ITS TERRITORY which, on this side, might be made." * *

* * * " It being necessary to provide the Government with soldiers, * * * you shall be very particular in recruiting people, * * * sending private agents to the territory of Costa Rica, *where, by no means, any armed force should enter*, unless with the written permission of the *commanding officers* of the different posts protecting the frontier of that Republic." * * *

The frontier spoken of in these instructions is the one drawn by the treaty of limits of 1858, and the commanding officers of the different posts of the Costa Rican frontier were those of the posts established to watch over the San Cárlos and Sarapiqui rivers as far as their confluence with the San Juan.

The treaty had, therefore, in the eyes of the Government of Nicaragua, perfect efficiency.

In contrast with the *firmness* now shown by Nicaragua to maintain the invalidity of the treaty of limits, Costa Rica must show the persistence with which, before she withdrew her adherence to the Ayón-Chevalier contract, the contrary opinion was maintained and carried into practical effect by the same Republic. It is for that reason that I have mentioned the three facts above stated.

On the other hand, it is worth while to notice here that the eagerness with which, subsequent to 1872, the validity of the treaty of limits has been denied in Nicaragua, says nothing in favor of the pretensions of that Government, nor weakens in the least the force of its previous contrary action. Admissions cannot be retracted.

And as the defense of Nicaragua wishes to find in the always firm and never contradictory action of the Government of Costa Rica some support of the conclusions adverse to the treaty which it formulates, it alleges the fact that Costa Rica acceded in good-will, and on several occasions, to give an amicable solution to the annoying question debated between the two countries ever since 1872, and cites especially the conference held at Managua, and the treaty made at that city on July 26th instant, where an indirect acknowledgment of the imperfection of the treaty of limits is alleged to be found.

The Treaty of Managua reads as follows:

" ARTICLE 1. The Government of Nicaragua *withdraws* the objections made to the validity of the treaty of limits with the Government of Costa Rica, signed on April 15, 1858, since it will obtain from Congress ON ITS PART (the part of the Government of Nicaragua) the second ratification which it (the Government of Nicaragua) has maintained to be indispensable.

The substance of this Article recognizes and proclaims, in a solemn and categorical manner, the justice of the cause which, during so many years, Costa Rica had been defending. No other meaning can be given to the *withdrawal* made by the Government of Nicaragua of the objections it had made against the treaty.

And, as after so many years of Nicaragua's having maintained that a second ratification of the treaty was necessary in order to cause her to consider herself bound by it, it was not possible that she should herself retract this point of mere form, nor was it advisable for Costa Rica that any formality which Nicaragua, whether right or wrong, thought necessary to protect the treaty against new objections, should be omitted, it is not to be wondered at that the said ratification should have been mentioned in the final part of Article I of the treaty of Managua; but this ratification was spoken of not as being a necessary formality asked for by Costa Rica, but as one considered by Nicaragua to be indispensable, although, in point of fact, it was not. The treaty of Managua could refer not to one or two ratifications of the treaty of 1858, but to as many as Nicaragua should like to consider necessary to acknowledge herself bound without danger of new retractations. This did not imply that Costa Rica accepted the necessity of such formalities.

If the treaty of Managua had reached its consummation, Nicaragua would have had the satisfaction to ratify for the sixth time, if I am not mistaken, the treaty of 1858, while Costa Rica, on her part, would have experienced the one of seeing, finally and forever, settled her difference with Nicaragua, through the withdrawal, by the latter, of the objections made by her to the treaty of limits.

It is, therefore, inconceivable how the treaty of Managua could have been spoken of in the defense of Nicaragua. If that instrument expresses the right criterion of the Nicaraguan Government, it furnishes the most eloquent testimony to the fact that, substantially, and laying aside this or that formality, the treaty of limits is valid, and not only valid but useful and profitable for Nicaragua.

CHAPTER XII.

IMPORTANCE OF THE DOCUMENTS REFERRED TO IN THIS CHAPTER FOR DE-
STROYING THE EFFECT OF THE PERSISTENCE WITH WHICH NICARAGUA
HAS MAINTAINED, EVER SINCE 1872, THE NON-VALIDITY OF THE TREATY OF
LIMITS.

THE Government of Nicaragua having boasted of its persistence, ever since 1872, in maintaining that the treaty of limits
of 1858 is not binding upon it, and it having formulated, also,
the charge of inconsistency against the Government of Costa
Rica, it does not seem inopportune to set forth here, as briefly
as possible, the substance of certain documents which I appended to my Argument, and of others which I append to the
present Reply, and show plainly thereby the truth of the facts.

Documents Nos. 23, 24, and 29, dated the first on May 16,
1858, the second and third on June 27 of the same year, and
the fourth on January 25, 1861; and those marked 31, 34,
and 35, dated, respectively, on April 1, May 26, and July 5,
1863, appended to the Argument of Costa Rica, will show
to the Arbitrator that Costa Rica exercised during that extensive period of time, not only without opposition, but at the
request of Nicaragua, the rights recognized to her by Article
VIII of the treaty in regard to intervention in grants of transit
and canal.

Documents Nos. 43 and 45 of the same Argument, dated,
respectively, May 26 and July 31, 1864, will also show to him
that Costa Rica, six years after the date of the treaty, was exercising sovereign rights over the territory of the right bank
of the San Juan river, and making explorations therein in order
to build a better and shorter road from the interior of the
country to the river bank.

Those marked Nos. 37, 40, 41, 42, 43, 44, 45, 46, 47, 48,
49, 50, 51, 53, and 55 in the Appendix to the present Reply,
equally show the exercise by Costa Rica of her sovereign

rights over the territory which, according to the treaty of 1858, belongs to her.

Document No. 47, of June 26, 1866, will show specially how emphatic was the protest of the Government of Costa Rica, which the Government of Nicaragua accepted as just, against the attempt to increase the volume of the waters of the lower part of the San Juan river at the expense of the Colorado river, which belongs to Costa Rica.

Document No. 50, dated January 25, 1867, will show also that Costa Rica, nine years after the conclusion of the treaty, carried it into execution, with the consent of Nicaragua, by establishing a sanitary cordon at a place of the frontier which the said treaty had marked out.

Document No. 51 of November 25, 1868, will show in the same manner that Costa Rica, ten years after the treaty, was exercising the rights which the said treaty recognized to her over the San Juan river.

Document No. 56 of July 22, 1872, will give testimony of the most eloquent character to the manner with which the Costa Rican Government listened to the so-called "doubts," which, then, for the first time, after 14 years of uninterrupted observance, arose in Nicaragua as to the validity of the treaty.

Document No. 58, dated December 3, 1875, will give an instance of the manner in which Costa Rica, seventeen years subsequent to the date of the treaty, continued to exercise her rights over the whole territory which that convention had given her.

And finally, documents Nos. 59 and 60, respectively dated on June 26, 1880, and September 10, 1886, will show, the former, how Costa Rica, twenty-two years after the date of the treaty, protested against the non-compliance in regard to her of the provisions of Article VIII of the same treaty, in the matter of the company organized in New York under the title of "Provisional Company of Interoceanic Canal," and the latter, the acceptance by Costa Rica of the explanations made by the Government of Nicaragua for the non-compliance with said provisions.

It is seen, therefore, from all of this, that since the month of May, 1858, to the month of September, 1886, Costa Rica has not receded one jot from her position in maintaining the efficiency and validity of the treaty to which she signed her name, and which on her part she always complied with faithfully and religiously.

CONCLUSION.

CONCLUSION.

BEFORE closing the present reply, the defense of Costa Rica deems it advisable to present a general summing up of its contents, which it submits as follows:

Under the arbitration treaty made at Guatemala, no possibility exists for the making of two awards, one deciding the principal question, and another, subsequent in date, on supplementary or secondary points suggested by Nicaragua. Both subjects must be the matter of one and the same decision.

The time for presentation of doubtful points, granted by the treaty of Guatemala, having been allowed by Nicaragua to pass unavailed, she cannot now be permitted to present those points, nor is Costa Rica bound to accept them as forming a part of the question submitted to arbitration.

All Royal Ordinances and Letters-Patent issued by the Spanish Kings, as well as all opinions of writers on the history of the Indies, are not, nor can they be, admitted in the present controversy, except as simply illustrating the historical precedents of the question, because the original rights of the parties were actually modified by subsequent transactions, as, for instance, the annexation of Guanacaste to Costa Rica, which took place, as all others, after the independence from Spain had been secured.

This is neither the proper time nor the proper place to make any declaration whatsoever, affecting questions not at issue, and neither debated nor submitted, as for instance the one referring to the determination of the limits between Costa Rica and Nicaragua, should the treaty of April 15, 1858, be adjudged void.

The *uti possidetis* of 1821 has nothing to do with the present question, because the subject under discussion is not the territorial extent of either Costa Rica or Nicaragua, independently of the treaty of April 15, 1858.

And notice must be taken of the fact that, although the doctrine of the *uti possidetis* of 1821 is in general correct, it is not so always in all cases and under all circumstances, but admits of modification under other rights of possession.

Had that doctrine been absolute and indisputable, Chiapas and Soconusco would have belonged to Guatemala until 1883, Sonsonate would belong to-day to the same Republic, &c., &c. The real and true *uti possidetis* is the one of 1838, when the federal bond was dissolved. The status which, as far as possession was concerned, existed at that time, and not the one existing in 1821, served as basis for the organization of the five Sovereign Republics of Central America.

The defense of Nicaragua considers that the treaty of limits of 1858 is a special one; but notice must be taken that, as far as requisites and formalities in regard to the manner of its conclusion are concerned, there is no difference at all that can be admitted between it and any other treaty whatsoever, since it was, as all others are, negotiated and concluded by plenipotentiaries appointed by the Executive, approved by the Executive, ratified by the Legislative, and exchanged and promulgated by the Executive.

This is the regular order of proceedings in use in all nations in regard to treaties; and the assertion can be made confidently that there is not a single precedent authorizing the course of proceedings, which according to the defense of Nicaragua the treaty of 1858 ought to have gone through, and which is, no doubt, a novelty in the Law of Nations.

If the treaty of limits is in any way special, it is so only in one respect, to wit: that while all public treaties are by their own nature permanent, for it is upon them that the peace of the nations therein concerned rest, and while all of them when once concluded cannot be allowed to fall, easily, or on light reasons, and much less for alleged informalities, never spoken of until after both contracting parties have been for years executing it, such a fate has not befallen, however, the treaty of limits.

The treaty of limits of 1858 was not concluded, approved, ratified, exchanged, and carried into effect under the sway of the Constitution of 1838, but under the sway of a transitory exceptional dictatorial regime, in which the National Constitutional Assembly excercised without limitation all the powers of the nation.

The laws under whose empire the treaty was made were the decrees of December 1, 1857, and February 5, 1858, the próvisions of which were literally complied with.

There is no conflict between the treaty of limits and the Constitution of 1838.

(a.) Because the Constitution of 1838 did not include the District of Nicoya within the territory of Nicaragua, since, as stated by the former Nicaraguan Constitution of April 8, 1826, the said District did not belong to her.

(*b.*) Because the Constitution of 1838 did not either include the territory south of the San Juan river, because said river was the limit clearly defined by the plain provisions of the Costa Rican Constitution of 1825 for the sovereignty of Costa Rica.

(*c.*) Because the settlement of 1858 had been foreseen by the said Constitution of 1838, wherein it was provided that as soon as such settlement should be reached it was to be understood as being embodied in the Constitution itself.

(*d.*) Because the Constitution of 1838 was not the fundamental law by which the perfection of the treaty should be governed.

•

Costa Rica maintains that the treaty of 1858 is as much an international convention as any other whatsoever; and as Nicaragua maintains that it is an amendment of the Constitution the burden of proof falls upon her. She has not produced it, nor can she do so, since the very first of all her laws on the matter, the foundation and source of them all, which is the Constitution of 1826, declares that the District of Nicoya does not form part of Nicaragua.

Supposing that the Nicaraguan Constitution of 1838 should have declared that the District of Guanacaste and the territory south of the San Juan river belonged to that Republic, a declaration which was never made, the effect thereof could never prevail against the fundamental laws of Costa Rica, which were previous—one of January 21, 1825, and the other the annexation of Nicoya of December 9th of the same year.

Ever since April 8, 1826, the date of the first Constitution of Nicaragua, that State may have had more or less reason upon which to set forth a claim to sovereignty over Guanacaste ; but she had no reason whatever to declare that the said District was included in her territory.

If the doctrines maintained by Nicaragua in her Argument should be admitted, scarcely one single treaty of limits could possibly stand. Which of them has not wounded in some way or another the real or alleged sovereignty of either of the parties ? Which one has ever been submitted to the special course of proceedings provided for constitutional amendments?

If the treaty of limits has to fall because Article 194 of the Constitution of 1838 was not complied with, its fall will drag down with it the whole political reconstruction of Nicaragua accomplished by the Assembly of 1858. Article 194 was not taken into consideration at all for the purposes of that reconstruction, although, under Article 196 of the same instrument, the former Article ought to have been followed in a general reform of the Constitution.

The first Costa Rican Constitution has been cited to prove that Guanacaste does not form part of Costa Rica; but no notice has been taken of the fact that the annexation of Guanacaste to Costa Rica took place ten months and eighteen days subsequent to the date of that Constitution. The Constitution was promulgated on January 28, 1825; and the annexation of Guanacaste was made by Federal decree of December 9 of the same year.

If such a ratification as the one asked for is wanting, there are no less than four or five subsequent ratifications given by different Nicaraguan Legislatures.

The whole of the present question is narrowed down to the proper construction of this phrase: "The Constituent Assembly of Nicaragua, in use of its legislative powers, &c., &c.," and whether the use of the word "legislative" is proper or improper: but, in good faith, that word cannot be understood to mean anything different from the desire that the treaty should produce such effects as those intended by the contracting parties.

The validity of the treaty has been repeatedly recognized by several Cabinets of Nicaragua between 1858 and 1872; but the change of mind that has been experienced in that Republic since 1872, under color of *doubts*, does not deprive the said acknowledgments of their efficiency.

The treaty of limits was negotiated, concluded, and perfected at a time in which Nicaragua was in full and perfect peace, Nicaragua being in possession and enjoyment of her lands, waters, ports, towns. &c.

Even granting that the treaty of limits involved alienation of territory, that alienation could be made under the Constitution of 1838, by the Assembly of 1858, or by any other legislative body, without any previous amendment of the fundamental law.

The Assembly of 1858 gave to the treaty of limits the character of a treaty, and not that of an amendment to the Constitution. And now it is too late to oppose the authentic interpretation made by the Constituent Legislator of Nicaragua, and which, like all interpretations of its kind, is a law of the State.

The failure of the accessory does not destroy the principal; and the treaty of limits cannot fail because the guarantee of Salvador is wanting. Such a guarantee was not essential to the treaty.

The guarantee of Salvador was not the only consideration, or the principal one, which led Nicaragua to bind herself. Such a guarantee did not form a part of the consideration.

The stipulation of Article X of the treaty never was a right for Nicaragua and a burden for Costa Rica, but a stipulation of mutual effect for and against both parties.

The Government of Costa Rica has always complied in good faith with the treaty of limits, and no act can be cited performed by it which reveals hesitation or doubt as to its validity. If it has permitted the efficiency of that treaty to be doubted in Nicaragua, and if it has endeavored to smooth the differences arising out of that action, that does not argue against the intimate conviction entertained by Costa Rica of the justice of her cause, but only shows once more her traditional policy of peace and concord with the other nations of Central America, and especially Nicaragua.

The treaty of limits was embodied in the Nicaraguan Constitution of 1858.

The treaty of limits has been respected up to the present time as a *status quo* in spite of the present controversy; and it is agreed that it shall be the *status quo* until all the questions pending between the two countries are finally settled.

If the treaty of 1858 falls, Costa Rica recovers thereby her ancient, historical, and legitimate limits of the La Flor and the Sapoá rivers, the lake, and the San Juan river.

I have thus far given the general recapitulation of this reply.

I must now add a few words about a point of special importance, that is, the one relative to the authenticity of the numerous documents appended to my Argument and to the present Reply, or which have been quoted in both of them. To file them all in the original, or in authenticated copies thereof, within such a short time as that granted for the preparation of both arguments would have been little short of a physical impossibility, besides being unnecessary. It is an impossibility, because many of those papers are in the Archives of Spain, the Mother Country, or in those of the ancient capital of the Kingdom of Guatemala; and it is unnecessary, because they all have been recently published.

In regard to the documents not in those Archives, and which are found in collections of laws and official newpapers, both of Costa Rica and Nicaragua, they are in my possession, either in the original printing or certified copies.

The defense of Costa Rica vouches for the authenticity of all the documents which it has presented or quoted, and will exhibit the originals or authenticated copies of those which the Arbitrator may be pleased to designate, should he deem it necessary.

It also holds at the disposal of the Arbitrator all the books that it has cited.

In conclusion, perhaps it may not be out of place to refer to the opinion of one of the most conspicuous men of Nicaragua, General Máximo Jerez, who, when the question about the treaty of limits began to be agitated in that country, expressed himself in the Nicaraguan Senate in the following language:

"From the beginning of this question on the validity or nullity of the treaty of limits of 1858, I always thought that we are on the wrong side. It always seemed to me that the reasons now alleged against the construction which we place upon the Nicaraguan laws at the time of the treaty are good at the most, and this is granting too much, to render that construction doubtful; and, under these circumstances, I never shall deem it proper for the public authorities of Nicaragua to declare, in the face of the world, and for the purpose of nullifying that treaty, that they, like children, did not understand their own laws, nor were bound to know what they meant.

"It is perhaps through a feeling analogous to the one I have just expressed that, although the Executive a long time ago submitted to the consideration of Congress the unfortunate question of the nullity of the treaty of limits, Congress has remained silent, and allowed the treaty exchanged in 1858, and executed in good faith during fifteen years, to continue in observance."[1]

The defense of Costa Rica has nothing to add to the preceding words of the Nicaraguan Senator, General Jerez, and confines itself to respectfully await such decision as the learned and upright Arbitrator shall be pleased to pass on the question.

PEDRO PÉREZ ZELEDÓN,

Envoy Extraordinary and Minister
Plenipotentiary of Costa Rica.

WASHINGTON, D. C.,
December 2, 1887.

---

[1] Apuntamientos Geográficos, Estadísticos é Históricos por Joaquin Bernardo Calvo. San José de Costa Rica, 1886. Imprenta Nacional 1887, page 18.

7

DOCUMENTS.

DOCUMENTS.

No. 1.

Royal Ordinance of February 10, 1576, *for the reduction of the Province of Taguzgalpa, situated to the north of the San Juan de Nicaragua river.*[1]

THE KING,

To the President, and the Judges of our Royal Audiencia, sitting at the city of Santiago, of the Province of Guatemala :

It has been represented to us on the part of Captain Diego Lopez, a resident of the city of Truxillo, of the Province of Honduras, that it is advisable and very necessary for the service of God our Lord, and that of ourselves, that the Province of Taguzgalpa, also called New Cartago, which is in the said Province, should be conquered and peopled by Spaniards ; that many years ago the city named Elgueta was founded there and peopled, but had to be abandoned owing to the inability of its inhabitants to resist the strong attacks of the natives ; and that he, the said Diego Lopez, would undertake, if we were pleased to accede to it, the said conquest and peopling, within four years, and at his own expense, provided that he would be granted the same favors that were granted to Captain Diego de Artieda, to whom we entrusted the discovery and settlement of the Province of Costa Rica ; and whereas all of this has been heard and considered in our Council of the Indies, and the said Council resolved that we might issue this, our

[1] From Colección de Documentos inéditos relativos al descubrimiento, conquista y organización de las antiguas posesiones españolas de América y Oceania, sacadas de los Archivos del Reyno y muy especialmente del de Indias. Competentemente autorizada. Vol. xiv, pages 528 to 537.

present ordinance, to which we have been pleased to accede: We do, therefore, command you to enter, as soon as this ordinance reaches you, into an agreement with the said Diego Lopez for the aforesaid purposes, observing the requisites provided for in the " Instructions " and ordinances in force relating to new settlements. And as soon as the said agreement is entered into, and before it is carried into execution, you shall submit it to us, together with your opinion about it, addressed to our Council aforesaid, to provide and decide as advisable.

Given at Madrid on February 10, 1576.

I, THE KING.

By command of His Majesty.

ANTONIO de ERASSO.

By virtue of the foregoing ordinance, an agreement for the conquest of Taguzgalpa was made in Guatemala, between Licentiate Palacio, an Associate Justice of the Audiencia, commissioned to that effect, and the said Diego Lopez; and the limits of the Province were marked as follows:

Firstly. His Majesty will appoint him his Governor and Captain-General of the said Province, which is the whole land included between the mouth of El Desaguadero, from its northern bank, and Cape Camaron, at the point where the Province of Honduras begins, with all the country included therein, until reaching the boundary and jurisdiction of the Province of Nicaragua and Nueva Segovia, and what is that of Honduras; and the said Captain Diego Lopez shall have the said Governorship during his lifetime, with the salary of two thousand ducats, to be paid from the Treasury or revenues belonging to His Majesty in the said Province; but if no such funds should exist, His Majesty shall not be bound to pay anything on account of that salary; and after the death of said Diego Lopez, his eldest son or son-in-law, as his heir, shall succeed him in this grant, provided that he is a person having the necessary qualifications and being His Majesty pleased to accept.

No. 2.

The President of the Royal Audiencia of Guatemala transmits to the Governor, and to the most Noble Corporation of the city of Cartago, a resolution, by which the election of members of the Spanish Cortes for Costa Rica and Nicoya was ordered to be made at that city.—It appears from this document that the District of Nicoya had actually been annexed to Costa Rica ever since May, 1813, about EIGHT YEARS before the independence from the mother country.

A preparatory meeting having been held ,the following resolution was passed:

Whereas, upon the reading of the official letter addressed to His Excellency the President by the Most Noble Corporation of the city of Cartago, it appears that the population of Costa Rica is alleged to be only 41,000 inhabitants, EVEN INCLUDING THE DISTRICT OF NICOYA, WHICH HAS BEEN ANNEXED TO COSTA RICA, which is less than the total which the Constitution requires, and that for this reason the said Governor and Council request that for the purposes of electing two members of Congress the said Province of Costa Rica should be united to the one of Leon, of Nicaragua, or that the districts of Masaya and Nicaragua (Rivas) should be incorporated into her ;

And whereas the Most Noble Council of the city of Leon reported adversely, on the grounds that the purposes had in view by Cartago were simply to alleviate the burden of taxes weighing upon it, and cause some other districts belonging to Nicaragua to share that burden, and that the present member of Congress for the said Province Don Florentino Castillo, had stated in an official letter addressed by him to His Excellency the President on June 8, 1812, that the same Council of the city of Cartago in its instructions to him had admitted the fact that the population of Costa Rica was about 70,000 inhabitants, and that even subtracting the natives of Africa, fortunately very few there, there would still remain about sixty thousand people of the other classes.

And whereas the said Most Noble Council of the city of Leon further represented that in case that the population of Costa Rica was not large enough, the District of Nicoya, which was bordering upon her, might be attached to her;

And whereas due consideration has been taken of ALL THE OTHER REASONS AND GROUNDS UPON WHICH IT WAS ORDERED THAT THE SAID DISTRICT OF NICOYA, UNITED TO COSTA RICA, SHOULD ELECT IN THE LATTER ONE MEMBER OF CONGRESS TO REPRESENT IN THE CORTES THE TWO LOCALITIES, AND PROMOTE THERE THE WELFARE OF THEIR WORTHY INHABITANTS;

And whereas no exact census has been made, showing any error in the approximate calculation made by this Assembly (Junta) upon the data and information on record;

And whereas the resolution which ordered that the election for one Member of Congress should take place at the capital of Costa Rica has proved beneficial to that Province, worthy to a great degree of the attentions of the government, and frees her people from the troubles and expense of a trip to Leon, many leagues distant, for the purposes of the said election,

Ordered, That the decision of this Board (Junta) be carried out, and that in consequence thereof the elections for Member of Congress be made under and according to the instructions enacted by this Board."

And this I communicate to you for your knowledge, and for such compliance therewith as may be incumbent upon you.

May God preserve you many years.

Guatemala, May 3, 1813.

BUSTAMANTE.

To the Governor and the Most Noble Council
of the City of Cartago.

No. 3.

The first Constituent Congress of Costa Rica directs that the Districts of Nicoya and Santa Cruz should be considered as temporarily annexed to the State, and protected as such.

The Constitutent Congress, in answer to your communication of the 30th of last month, wherein, by order of the Supreme Chief Magistrate, you ask for instructions as to what must be done with the District of Nicoya, resolved at the meeting held yesterday, as follows: That the Districts of Nicoya and Santa Cruz must be considered *annexed* to this State *ad interim*, until otherwise decided finally by the High Powers, and that therefore the said districts must be protected and taken care of with as much circumspection, prudence, and earnestness as might be granted to any other integral part of the Costa Rican State.

And by order of Congress, and returning to you the papers of the case, we transmit the above to you for your information and the proper effects.

God, Union, and Liberty.

San José, January 29, 1825.

MANUEL FERNANDEZ,
Secretary.
MANUEL ALVARADO,
Secretary.

To The Citizen Secretary-General *pro tem.*

No. 4.

Measures taken by the Constitutional Assembly of Costa Rica to carry into execution the Federal Decree which annexed the District of Nicoya to her own Territory.

ORDER.

OFFICE OF THE SECRETARIES
OF THE CONSTITUTIONAL ASSEMBLY.

To The Citizen Minister-General :

The Assembly having been made acquainted with the terms of the Federal Decree, DECLARING THAT THE DISTRICT OF NICOYA BE ANNEXED TO THIS STATE—

Resolved, That the Executive, in compliance therewith, shall cause the said District to be furnished, as soon as possible, with all the necessary officers; that the different branches of the administration of its Government shall be organized there in the proper manner; that THE CONSTITUTION AND THE LAWS OF THE STATE shall be communicated to it and enforced ; and that a census, as approximate as possible, of the population of the said District shall be made and sent to the Assembly in order that it may resolve about the representation to be given the District in that body, and the manner of election.

And by order of the Assembly we transmit the above to you for the information of the Chief Magistrate.

God, Union, and Liberty.

San José, April 14, 1826.

PEDRO ZELEDÓN,
Secretary.

FRANCISCO MARIA OREAMUNO,
Secretary.

No. 5.

Extracts from the Constitution of the State of Nicaragua of April 8, 1826, showing that at that time the District of Guanacaste or Nicoya was not an integral part of the State, but had been, by its own will, and with the sanction of the Federal Power, annexed to the bordering State of Costa Rica.

In the presence of God, the Author and Supreme Legislator of the Universe:

We, the Representatives of the people of Nicaragua in Constituent Assembly convened, being fully and lawfully authorized *by our constituents,* and by the Federal Compact of the Republic, to enact an organic law which may secure the prosperity and happiness of the State, consisting in the perfect enjoyment of the rights of man and citizen, namely, liberty, equality, safety, and property, have hereby decreed and sanctioned the following political Constitution:

TITLE FIRST.

Of the State, its Territory, its Rights, and its Duties.

CHAPTER I.

Of the State and its Territory.

ARTICLE 1. THE STATE shall retain the name of STATE OF NICARAGUA. It consists of all its inhabitants; and it forms part of the Central American Confederation.

ARTICLE II. THE TERRITORY OF THE STATE EMBRACES THE DISTRICTS OF NICARAGUA, GRANADA, MANAGUA, MASAYA, MATAGALPA, SEGOVIA, LEON, SUBTIABA, AND EL REALEJO.[1]

Its limits are: On the east, the Sea of the Antilles; on the

---

[1] The District of Nicoya was not named in this description. It had been segregated from Nicaragua and incorporated into Costa Rica two years before.

north, the State of Honduras; on the west, the Gulf of Conchagua; on the south, the Pacific Ocean; and on the south-east, the free State of Costa Rica.

ARTICLE III. THE ABOVE-NAMED TERRITORY SHALL BE DIVIDED into Departments, and a special law, providing for the number and limits thereof, shall be enacted.

*   *   *   *   *   *

ARTICLE CLXVIII. The present Constitution is solemnly sanctioned by this Constituent Assembly.

Given in the City of Leon, on April 8th, 1826.

MANUEL MENDOZA,
Deputy for Matagalpa, President.

ISIDRO REYES,
Deputy for Leon, Vice-President.

PEDRO MUÑOZ,
Deputy for Nicaragua.

RAMON PACHECO,
Deputy for Subtiaba.

GREGORIO PARRAS,
Deputy for El Realejo.

SILVESTRE SELVA,
Deputy for Granada.

FRANCISCO REÑASCO,
Deputy for Masaya.

JUAN JOSÉ ZAVALA,
Deputy for Managua.

JOSÉ VICENTE MORALES,
Deputy (substitute) for Leon.

JUAN MANUEL ZAMORA,
Deputy for Masaya.

FRANCISCO PARRALES,
Deputy for Nicaragua, Secretary.

SEBASTIAN ESCOVAR,
Deputy for Granada, Secretary.[1]

---

[1] As was natural and logical Nicoya was not represented in the Constituent Assembly of Nicaragua.

Leon, *April* 22, 1826.

Let it be executed.

Given under my hand, sealed with the seal of the State and countersigned by the Secretary in charge, *ad interim*, of all the Departments of the Government.

JOSÉ MIGUEL DE LA QUADRA.
JUAN ARGÜELLO,
Secretary.

No. 6.

Schedule showing the way in which the districts of the State of Costa Rica should elect their deputies.

The letter " A " indicates the place where the parochial electors should meet for the election of the district electors; and the letter " B " indicates the place where the district electors must meet to elect the deputies and their substitutes, and also the persons who must exercise the supreme powers of the State.

	ELECTORS.			
Districts.	Parochial.	District.	Deputies.	Substitutes.
San José.	San José. A. B.	3		
	Curridabat,	1	11	3	1
Population, 16,288.	Aserri,	1		
Cartago.	Cartago. A. B.	22		
	Coó,	1		
	Quircot,	1	8	2	1
Population, 12,330.	Tobosi,	1		
	Tres Rios,	1		
Heredia.	Heredia. A. B.	22		
Population, 12,260.	Barba,	3	8	2	1
Alajuela.	Alajuela. A. B.	16	5		
Population, 8,027.				
Bagaces.	Cañas. A.	1		2	1
	Bagaces,	1	1	
Population, 1,444.	Esparza,	1		
Escacú.	Escacú. A. B.	5	3	1	0
Population, 3,273.	Pacaca,	2		
Ujarraz.	Ujarraz. A. B.	3		
	Olosi,	2	2		
Population, 2,605.	Cucurrique,	1		1	0
Térraba.	Térraba. A.	2	1		
Population, 1,019.	Boruca,	1		
Nicoya.	Santa Cruz. A. B.	3		
	Nicoya,	3	3	1	0
Population, 4,600.	Guanacaste,	3		

San José, September 28, 1826.

CASTRO,
Secretary.
OREAMUNO,
Proto Secretary.

No. 7.

The District of Nicoya called to take part in the election of the Supreme Federal Authorities, by order of the Congress of Costa Rica, and as an integral part of the latter State.

The Supreme Chief Magistrate of the free State of Costa Rica,

Whereas the Assembly has decreed and the Council sanctioned what follows:

The Constitutional Assembly of the free State of Costa Rica, in compliance with Title III of the Federal Constitution, as far as the DISTRICT OF NICOYA, NEWLY INCORPORATED INTO THIS STATE by decree of the Federal Congress of December 9, 1825, is concerned, has been pleased to decree and decrees:

ARTICLE 1. The District of Nicoya shall take part in the election of the Supreme Federal authorities in the Western Department of this State by choosing the electors to represent it in the Electoral College.

ARTICLE 2. The schedule hereto appended shall designate the share of representation to be given to each district and town for the election aforesaid; and the schedule appended to the decree of October 13th of last year is hereby repealed. In everything else the election shall be conducted according to the provision of that decree.

To THE REPRESENTATIVE COUNCIL.

Given at San José, on September 29, 1826.

PEDRO ZELEDÓN,
President.

JOSÉ ANTONIO CASTRO,
Secretary.

FRANCISCO MARIA OREAMUNO,
Proto Secretary.

HALL OF THE COUNCIL,
San José, *October* 6, 1826.

Let it pass to the Executive.

JOSÉ RAFAEL DE GALLEGOS,
President.

GREGORIO HERRERO,
Secretary.

Therefore let it be executed.
San José, October 10, 1826.

JUAN MORA.

To Citizen MANUEL AGUILAR.

No. 8.

Nicoya is granted the right to take part in the election of the Supreme Authorities of the State of Costa Rica according to the Constitution thereof.

The Supreme Chief Magistrate of the free State of Costa Rica,

Whereas the Assembly has decreed and the Council sanctioned what follows:

The Constitutional Assembly of the free State of Costa Rica, considering that the District of Nicoya, AGAIN ANNEXED TO THIS STATE, ought to be ruled according to the Constitution, and to have such popular representation as provided by the same, has been pleased to decree, and does hereby decree, as follows:

ARTICLE I. The District of Nicoya shall be at once represented in the Constitutional Assembly by one Deputy, who shall be elected by the people, to serve this year and the next one of 1827.

ARTICLE II. The said District shall take part at the proper time in the election of the Supreme Powers of the State; and for that purpose three votes shall be allotted to it.

ARTICLE III. The elections shall take place as provided by the Decree of the Constituent Congress of January 21, 1825, and by the schedule appended thereto, as now amended by the addition of the said District.

To THE REPRESENTATIVE COUNCIL.

Given at San José on September 28, 1826.
PEDRO ZELEDÓN,
President.
JOSÉ ANTONIO CASTRO,
Secretary.
FRANCISCO MARIA OREAMUNO,
Secretary.

HALL OF THE COUNCIL,
SAN JOSÉ, *October* 6, 1826.

Let it be transmitted to the Executive.

JOSÉ RAFAEL DE GALLEGOS,
President.

GREGORIO HERRERO,
Secretary.

SAN JOSÉ, *October* 10, 1826.

Therefore let it be executed.

JUAN MORA.

To Citizen MANUEL AGUILAR.

No. 9.

The Nicaraguan territory ends at the La Flor river.

The Legislative Assembly of the State of Nicaragua, considering:—that the only road through which trade can be carried on between this State and the State of Costa Rica is exceedingly out of order,—that it is urgent to repair it in order to maintain and facilitate relations of commerce, friendship, and reciprocity,—and that energetic measures are required to accomplish this purpose, decrees:

ARTICLE I. The road between the *city of Rivas in Nicaragua and the District of Nicoya* shall be repaired, AS FAR AS THE RIVER CALLED LA FLOR.[1]

---

[1] Limit of the two States.

No. 10.

*The Constitutional Assembly of Costa Rica enacts several meas-
ures for the cultivation of certain lands belonging to the
State, situated on the right bank of the San Juan del Norte
river.*

The Supreme Chief Magistrate of the free State of Costa
Rica.

Whereas the Assembly has decreed, and the Council sanctioned, what follows :

The Constitutional Assembly of the free State of Costa Rica,
wishing to secure the welfare of the people and the prosperity
of the State, taking into consideration that a great many tracts
of land of considerable extent are found in it uncultivated and
uninhabited, and that as long as they remain in this condition
they are useless, while, on the contrary, if cultivated and settled they would produce much good ; wishing, therefore, to give
some impulse to beneficial enterprises in this direction, and
give some inducement by means of gratuitous grants of land to
those who should desire to undertake them, has been pleased
to decree, and does hereby decree, as follows :

Article I. All those who shall settle upon lands in the
north, northeast, east, and south, and cultivate them for five
consecutive years, shall be granted the whole tract cultivated
by them for the term of eight years, and also an additional
" caballeria ;"[1] and those who shall so engage themselves in
the cultivation of the land, or settle there, within two
years after the publication of this law, shall be given, in addition to the two rewards above named, one more " caballeria."

Article II. In addition to the rewards granted in the foregoing Article, one more " caballeria " shall be given to those

---

[1] Caballeria is a measure containing 45 hectareas, 25 areas, and 1§ square
meters (Metric System).

who shall engage themselves in cultivating cocoa, or in planting any kind of dye-wood.

ARTICLE III. Those who shall engage themselves upon said lands in the raising of horned cattle, starting with from 25 to 1,000 head, shall be granted a *sitio* (seven " caballerias ") of land ; and those starting with more than 1,000 head of cattle shall have two *sitios*, provided in both cases that the settlement is continued for five consecutive years ; and those who shall settle upon the lands within the next two years shall have three additional " caballerias."

ARTICLE IV. The favors granted by the Decree of July 14, 1825, are hereby extended to every product grown, raised, or obtained in the aforesaid settlements.

ARTICLE V. Every settler who should ask for the survey of his lands shall have his request granted, under the provisions of the Decree of May 27th ultimo ; and, if his petition is filed within two years after the publication of this law, the additional favor shall be granted to him by allowing the operation to be made by a Commissioner appointed by him, and sworn by the Intendente. The latter officer shall attend to everything else, including the issuing of the patent or title without charging any fee.

ARTICLE VI. The lands to be granted, on the north and northeast, shall be as follows : along the road to the city of Alajuela, BETWEEN THE NEIGHBORHOOD OF FRARJANES AND THE ISLAND AND THE SAN JUAN RIVER: along the road to San José BETWEEN THE NEIGHBORHOOD OF THE BLASCO AND SANTA ROSA RIVERS AND THE BANKS OF THE SAID SAN JUAN RIVER ; along the road to Coó, between the neighborhood of the El Pescado river and the volcano of Turialba and beyond it ; along the roads of Matina, between the Turialba river and the limits of Tucurrique and beyond it; and along the frontier of Colombia, between the mouth of the Santa Clara mountains and the border-line, this line being temporarily the one drawn from one of the two mentioned points to the other. On the south the Government shall in each case, as it presents itself. designate the tracts of land to be allotted between the Portalon lands and the El Naranjo river, and also between the mouths of the great rivers of the interior and La Candelaria, and between the PENINSULA OF NICOYA OR CABO BLANCO, and the mouths of the Alvarado river, between the Gulf and the neighborhood of Barco-Quebrado.

To the Representative Council.

Given at San José, this 26th day of October, 1828.

FELIX HIDALGO,
Vice-President.

JOSÉ ANTONIO CASTRO,
Secretary.

PEDRO DOBLEZ.
Proto Secretary.

HALL OF THE COUNCIL,
SAN JOSÉ, *November* 3, 1828.

Let it be transmitted to the Executive.

JOSÉ RAFAEL DE GALLEGOS,
President.

GREGORIO GUERRERO,
Secretary.

Therefore let it be executed.

San José, November 4, 1828.

JUAN MORA.

To Citizen JOAQUIN BERNARDO CALVO.

No. 11.

The village of Guanacaste is raised by the Government of Costa Rica to the category of a town.

The Supreme Chief Magistrate of the free State of Costa Rica,

Whereas the Assembly has decreed and the Council sanctioned what follows :

The Extraordinary Assembly of the free State of Costa Rica, considering the meritorious circumstances of the village of Guanacaste, its progress, and the increase of its population, has been pleased to decree, and does hereby decree, as follows :

ARTICLE I. The village of Guanacaste is raised to the category of a town.

ARTICLE II. The Executive shall issue the proper credential on stamped paper of the 2d class of seal No. 1.

Let it be transmitted to the Representative Council.

Given at San José on July 18, 1831.

JOSÉ GABRIEL DEL CAMPO,
President.

MANUEL ALVARADO,
Secretary.

RAFAEL OSEJO,
Secretary.

HALL OF THE COUNCIL,
SAN JOSÉ, *July* 23, 1831,

Let it be transmitted to the Executive.

BASILIO CARRILLO,
President.

JOSÉ ANSELMO SANCHO,
Secretary.

Therefore let it be executed.

San José, July 23, 1831.

JUAN MORA.

To the Citizen JOAQUIN BERNARDO CALVO.

No. 12.

The town of Santa Cruz (in the District of Nicoya) has a Representative in the Assembly of the State of Costa Rica.

The Supreme Chief Magistrate of the free State of Costa Rica, in pursuance of the provisions of Articles 51, 56, and 80 of the Constitution of the State, for the renovation in the coming year 1833, of the supreme legislative, executive, and conservative powers, has been pleased to decree, and does hereby decree, as follows:

The District Electoral College, to be appointed in January of next year (1833), for the renovation of members of the supreme powers of the State, shall act as follows: * *

7th. Santa Cruz shall retain the representation which, under the law of May 30, last year, it ought to have had.

*   *   *   *   *   *

Let it be transmitted to the Executive.

Given in San José on the 15th of May, 1832.

JOAQUIN DE IGLESIAS,
President.

NICOLAS ULLOA,
Secretary.

JOSÉ MARIA ARIAS,
Secretary.

Therefore let it be executed.

San José, May 18, 1832.

JUAN MORA.

To Citizen JOAQUIN BERNARDO CALVO.

No. 13.

Instructions given to the Special Commissioner of the Government of Costa Rica to visit the Districts of Nicoya and Bagaces.

The Supreme Chief Magistrate of the free State of Costa Rica :

Whereas one of the first duties of the Executive power is to keep order and preserve the tranquillity of the State, taking for that effect such measures as may be deemed advisable ; and whereas an official communication, dated on the 24th ultimo, from the Superior Court of Justice, and also several reports of the political authorities and of the Intendente, as well as reports from several trustworthy persons, have been received, all to the effect that the Districts of Nicoya and Bagaces are becoming demoralized, either for want of energy on the part of the local authorities and their failure to enforce the laws and superior orders, or owing to the insubordination which several emigrants from the State of Nicaragua have inculcated in their inhabitants ; and whereas, if the proper measure is not taken in time to preserve order in that precious part of the State, the result will be to endanger public safety and tranquillity, to cause all the elements of prosperity to remain stationery, if not to decline, and to subject the individual rights to the attacks of malice and lawlessness, and render the police either faulty or useless ; and whereas the lack of prompt knowledge on the part of the superior authority of what occurs in those districts renders it difficult for the Government to devise the proper means for enforcing the law and securing the happiness and welfare of the people ; and whereas, in consequence of the disorder therein prevalent, the public Treasury of that locality cannot get the means necessary for the support of the Government and the promotion of works of general interest, in spite of the meritorious circumstances as well as righteousness of the Intendente General of the State, Citizen Joaquin Rivas, I have therefore decided, in pursuance of Section 2d, Article LXXXII of the Organic Law, and of Articles XIII and XXXVII of the Rules and Regulations of September 23, 1831, to decree, and I do hereby decree, as follows :

1st. Citizen Joaquin Rivas, the Intendente General, is hereby appointed Commissioner, for the Executive, and in representation thereof, to go personally and as soon as possible to the Districts of Nicoya and Bagaces, and visit there with the zeal and activity characterizing him, all the villages and towns of both Districts, and do there and perform all that is provided for in this Decree and in the instructions which separately shall be given to him.

2d. The said Commissioner shall do and perform what Article 44 of the law of June 13, 1828, orders the superior political chief to do, and shall cause the municipal authorities to comply with all the laws communicated to them for the best order in the public administration, especially in matters of police, education, increase of the municipal revenue, honest collection and disbursement of the public funds, the public health, the protection of the social guarantees, and the preservation of the archives.

3d. The Commissioner shall also cause the Government's Decree of August 31, 1832, about vagrants and foreigners, to be strictly enforced ; and he shall not leave the town which he may be visiting without having caused all that has been provided for, to be put in practice and without having established in it primary schools.

4th. The Commissioner shall also, in pursuance of the laws in force, inspect the offices in charge of the sale of stamped paper ; and he shall also inform himself of the condition of the public revenue, and cause the laws establishing taxes of all kinds to be enforced, giving for that purpose to each subordinate such orders and instructions as may be required.

5th. The Commissioner shall report to the Government the

result of his action, for which purpose he shall keep such registers or journals as may be necessary; and, whenever he may deem it advisable, he shall communicate directly with the Government from the place where he might happen to be.

6th. The civil, military, and ecclesiastical authorities of the said Districts, and their towns and cities, shall receive and recognize the aforesaid Intendente as Commissioner of the Government for the purposes aforesaid, and shall pay him such respect and consideration as is due to his character.

7th. The salary of $30 per month shall be paid the said Commissioner, in addition to the one he receives under the law as Intendente General; and he shall be attended by two mounted orderlies.

8th. The present Decree shall be printed, published, and circulated for its due execution.

Given at the city of San José this 7th day of February, 1834.

JOSÉ RAFAEL DE GALLEGOS.

To The Secretary-General of the Government.

No. 14.

Classification of the towns of Costa Rica in reference to home government and Treasury matters.

The Vice-President acting as the Supreme Chief Executive Magistrate of the free State of Costa Rica.

Whereas the Assembly has decreed and the Council sanctioned the following:

"The Constitutional Assembly of the free State of Costa Rica, desiring to make the transaction of Government business expeditious and efficient, and also to improve the organization of the Treasury, by appointing three high officers, who shall exercise superior authority, with functions equal to those of the sub-delegates of the Intendencia General, in their respective districts, has decreed, and does hereby decree:—

ARTICLE I. In order to facilitate the administration of the Government, in matters of Police, and the Treasury, three high officers shall be stationed, one at Cartago, another at Alajuela, *and the third at the town of Guanacaste:* they shall have, in their respective districts, the same duties as the Political Chief had under the law of June 13, 1828; and they must have the qualifications required by the said law, which is hereby amended so as to be made applicable to them.

*　　*　　*　　*　　*　　*　　*

ARTICLE VI. The Departments or districts shall be named Eastern, Western, and Guanacaste: the first comprising the cities of San José and Cartago, the towns of Paraiso and Escasú and the villages of Curridabat, Aserri, Union, Quircót, Tobosi, Coó, Orosi, Tucurrique, Térraba, Boruca and the valleys of Turrialba and Matina; the second the cities of Heredia and Alajuela, the town of Barba and the villages of Pacaca, the Aguacate Mine, Esparza and Puntarenas; and the 3d *the towns*

OF GUANACASTE AND BAGACES, AND THE VILLAGES OF SANTA CRUZ, NICOYA AND CAÑAS.

Given in the city of Alajuela this 24th day of March, 1835.

MANUEL AGUILAR,
President.

RAFAEL REYES,
Secretary.

MANUEL ANTONIO BONILLA,
Secretary.

HALL OF THE COUNCIL,
ALAJUELA, *March* 26, 1835.

Let it pass to the Executive.

JOSÉ JULIAN BLANCO,
President.

JOSÉ MARIA ALVARADO,
Secretary.

Therefore let it be executed.

Alajuela, March 27th, 1835.

MANUEL FERNANDEZ.

To THE MINISTER GENERAL.

No. 15.

Guanacaste is declared to be one of the five judicial districts of Costa Rica.

The Vice-President, acting as the Supreme Chief Executive Magistrate of the free State of Costa Rica,

Whereas the Assembly has decreed and the Council sanctioned the following:

*　　*　　*　　*　　*　　*

Article VI. For the remainder of the year the five justices shall be judges of first instance for the five judicial districts in which the State is divided, namely: 1st, the District of Cartago, with the towns of Térraba, Boruca, Tucurrique, Orosi, Coó, Quircot, Tobosi, Valley de Matina, Paraiso, and La Union; 2d, the District of San José, with the towns of Curridabat, Aserri, Escasú, and Pacaca; 3d, the District of Heredia, with the town of Barba; 4th, the District of Alajuela, with the Aguacate mining lands; and, 5th, THE DISTRICT OF GUANACASTE, WITH BAGACES, CAÑAS, NICOYA, AND SANTA CRUZ.

To the Representative Council.

Given at the city of Alajuela on March 23, 1835.

MANUEL AGUILAR,
President.

RAFAEL REYES,
Secretary.

MANUEL ANTONIO BONILLA,
Secretary.

HALL OF THE COUNCIL,
ALAJUELA, *March* 27, 1835.

Let it pass to the Executive.

JOSÉ JULIAN BLANCO,
President.

JOSÉ MARIA ALVARADO,
Secretary.

Therefore let it be executed.

Alajuela, March 27, 1835.

MANUEL FERNANDEZ.

To THE MINISTER-GENERAL.

No. 16.

The faithfulness of the District of Nicoya, and its services subsequent to its incorporation to Costa Rica, are recognized and rewarded.

The Supreme Chief Magistrate of the free State of Costa Rica, taking into consideration THE SERVICES RENDERED BY THE DISTRICT OF NICOYA, AND THE FAITHFULNESS WITH WHICH IT HAS DISTINGUISHED ITSELF EVER SINCE ITS ANNEXATION TO THIS STATE, and desiring to facilitate by every possible means the increase of its population, as well as its commerce, and secure for it the degree of progress to which it is entitled by the good character of its inhabitants, the fertility of its soil, and its advantageous topographic position, has been pleased to decree, and decrees as follows :

ARTICLE I. An annual fair to last three days, to commence on December 8th of each year, is permitted to Guanacaste ; and also to Santa Cruz, to begin on Ascension day ; and also to the town of Nicoya, to begin on Candlemas day ; and also to the town of Bagaces, to begin on July 24th ; and also to the town of Cañas, to begin on December 25th. And the authorities of the said localities shall see, under their strictest responsibility, that public order and peace and public morality are not disturbed, and that the disturbers of public peace are duly punished according to law.

ARTICLE II. The ground on which the said fairs are to be held, and the house to be used for the same, whether already built or to be built in the future, is hereby granted to the inhabitants of said towns in fee simple, the area of the ground being equal to a $\frac{1}{30}$ yard lot of national measure.

ARTICLE III. The Government shall also see that the towns of the said Department are given possession of such grounds to be used as commons, as they are entitled to, and that by this means their own resources are increased, provided, however, that the formalities of the law applicable to the case are duly complied with.

To the Representative Council.

Given at the city of Heredia, on the 25th day of March, 1836.

MANUEL AGUILAR,
President.

MANUEL BONILLA,
Secretary.

FRANCISCO SAENZ,
Proto Secretary.

HALL OF THE COUNCIL,
HEREDIA, *April* 8, 1836.

Let it pass to the Executive.

JUAN V. ESCALANTE,
President.

JOSÉ MARIA ECHAVARRIA,
Secretary.

Therefore let it be executed.

San José, April 9, 1836.

BRAULIO CARRILLO.

To THE MINISTER-GENERAL.

No. 17.

The rank and title of City is given to the town of Guanacaste in recognition of the services rendered by it to the State by resisting the invasion of Manuel Quijano.

The Supreme Chief Magistrate of the free State of Costa Rica,

Whereas the Assembly has decreed and the Council sanctioned what follows:

The Constituent Assembly of the free State of Costa Rica considering—1st. THAT THE DEPARTMENT OF GUANACASTE has rendered an important service to the State in defending itself against the invaders of its territory under the leadership of Manuel Quijano.—2d. That it is necessary for the State to show in some way its appreciation of the said service and of the esteem in which it holds the inhabitants of that district for the courage and enthusiasm shown by them on that occasion, has been pleased to decree, and decrees as follows :

ARTICLE I. The rank and title of a City is granted to the town of Guanacaste.

ARTICLE II. The inhabitants of the whole Department are hereby exempted for one year from paying the tax known as " road tax."

To the Representative Council.

Given at the City of Heredia on August 25, 1836.

MANUEL ANTONIO BONILLA,
President.

FRANCISCO SAENZ,
Proto Secretary.

9

HALL OF THE COUNCIL,

Heredia, *September* 2, 1836.

Let it pass to the Executive.

JOAQUIN FLORES,

President.

JOSÉ MARIA ECHAVARRIA,

Secretary.

Therefore let it be executed.

San José, September 3, 1836.

BRAULIO CARRILLO.

To The Minister-General.

No. 18.

Schedule for the election of deputies to the Constituent Assembly of the State, at the rate of one deputy for each 5,000 souls, and fractions of that unit to the number of 3,000. The letter A. means the place where the parochial electors must meet, and the letter B. shows the place where the district electors must meet.

ELECTORS.

Districts.	Parochial Electors.		District Electors.	Deputies.	Substitutes.
Paraiso. Population, 3,825.	Paraiso. A. B.	3	4	1	0
	Matina,	1			
	Orosi,	1			
	Tucurrique,	1			
	Boruca,	1			
	Térraba. A.	2			
Cartago. Population, 15,875.	Cartago. A. B.	28	10	3	1
	Coó,	1			
	Quircot,	1			
	Tobosi,	1			
	Union,	1			
San José. Population, 20.262.	San José. A. B.	38	13	4	2
	Curridabat,	1			
	Aserri,	1			
Heredia. Population, 15,262.	Heredia. A. B.	27	10	3	1
	Barba,	3			
Alajuela. Population, 10,151.	Cañas. A.	1	6	3	1
	Alajuela. A. B. with Aguacate,	16			
	Bagaces,	1			
	Esparza and Punta Arenas,	1			
Escasú. Population, 3,513.	Escasú. A. B.	5	4	1	0
	Pacaca,	2			
Nicoya. Population, 5,846.	Guanacaste. A. B.	3	4	1	0
	Santa Cruz. A.	5			
	Nicoya,	4			

Office of the Secretary of the Assembly, San José, July 4, 1838.

JUAN BONILLA,
Secretary.

RAFAEL RAMIREZ,
Secretary.

No. 19.

The Constituent Assembly of Nicaragua of 1838 gives power to the Executive to enter into a treaty with the Envoy of Costa Rica.

The Chief Magistrate of the State of Nicaragua,

Whereas the Constituent Assembly has decreed as follows:

The Constituent Assembly of the State of Nicaragua, desiring to strengthen friendship and alliance with the State of Costa Rica, on the ground that the present safety and future happiness of both States depends to a great extent on the accomplishment of this desire, and considering that the Executive needs ample authority to deal with the Envoy accredited in this capital;—in use of the ample powers which have been vested in it by the people, has been pleased to decree and decrees:

The Executive is hereby authorized to adjust with the Envoy of Costa Rica such treaties of friendship and alliance as may be deemed conducive to the good of both States, subject to the approval of this Assembly [1]

Let it be transmitted to the Executive for the purposes that it be printed, published, and circulated.

Given at Leon, on November 8, 1838.

BENITO ROSALEZ,
President.

SEBASTIAN SALINAS,
Secretary.

FAUSTO CHAMORRO,
Secretary.

Therefore let it be executed.

Leon, December 1, 1838.

JOSÉ NUÑEZ.

To The Secretary-General.

---

[1] This decree was issued when Don Francisco Maria Oreamuno, Costa Rican Envoy, presented himself to the Cabinet of Nicaragua for the purpose that that State should finally give up her claim to the District of Guanacaste.

No. 20.

Law enacted by the Constituent Assembly of Nicaragua on December 21, 1838, to carry into effect Article 11 of the Constitution of the same year.

The Chief Magistrate of the State of Nicaragua,

Whereas the Constituent Assembly has decreed what follows:

The Constituent Assembly of the State of Nicaragua, desiring to establish and regulate the method of election of the Supreme authorities of the State in conformity with the rules prescribed by the organic law, has been pleased to decree and decrees:

CHAPTER I.

ARTICLE I. *The State is divided into four Departments,* namely, East, West, North, and South.

ARTICLE II. The Department of the East embraces three Districts, namely Granada, Masaya, Xinotepet.

ARTICLE III. The Department of the West embraces two, namely Leon and Chinandega.

ARTICLE IV. The Department of the North embraces two Districts, namely Segovia and Matagalpa.

ARTICLE V. THE DEPARTMENT OF THE SOUTH SHALL EMBRACE ONLY ONE, NAMELY RIVAS, UNTIL THE QUESTION PENDING BETWEEN THIS GOVERNMENT AND THE GOVERNMENT OF COSTA RICA FOR THE REINCORPORATION OF THE DISTRICT OF GUANACASTE IS SETTLED.

ARTICLE VI. The District of Granada consists of the city of the same name, the town of Acoyapa, and the villages of Boaco, Camoapa, Lustepet, Comalapa, Juigalpa, Lóvago and Loviguïsca.

ARTICLE VII. The District of Masaya consists of the city of this name and those of Managua and Tipitapa, and the towns of Nindirí and Mateare.

ARTICLE VIII. The District of Jinotepet consists of the village of this name and those of San Juan, Nandaimes, Santa Catarina. Niquinohomo, Masatepe, Diriá, Diriomo, Diriamba, Nandasmo, San Márcos, San Rafael and Santa Teresa.

The District of Leon consists of the city of this name and the towns Subtiaba, Pueblo Nuevo, and Nagarote.

ARTICLE X. The District of Chinandega consists of this town and those of Realejo and Villa Nueva, and the villages of El Viejo, Chichigalpa, Guadalupe, Posoltega, Posolteguilla, Telica, Quezalquaque, Somotillo, El Sauce and Santa Rosa.

ARTICLE XI. The District of Segovia consists of the villages of Somoto, Totogalpa, Ocotal, Mosonte, Macuelizo, Nueva Segovia, Jicaro, Jalapa, Telpaneca, Palacagüina, Jalagüina, Pueblo Nuevo, Condega, San Juan de Leinay, Estilé and La Trinidad.

ARTICLE XII. The District of Matagalpa consists of the village of the same name and those of San Rafael, Jinotega, Sébaco, Metapa, Tierra Bona, San Dionisio, Esquipulas, Minmui, and San Ramon.

ARTICLE XIII. The District of Rivas consists of the city of the same name and the villages of San Gorge, Pueblo Viejo, Buenos Ayres, Potosi, Obrage, Pueblo Nuevo, Tola, Ometepe and Moyogalpa.

ARTICLE XIV. Each District above named shall elect one deputy, but the District of Leon and the District of Rivas shall elect two each. The number of the primary electors which corresponds to each town or village above named shall appear from the schedule, which is appended to this decree.

ARTICLE XV. Those towns, where more than ten electors are to be chosen, shall be divided in as many cantons as are designated in the schedules appended to this decree, and the limits of these cantons shall be fixed by the respective municipal authorities according to the basis of their population and the number of the electors to be chosen. The same municipal authorities shall also designate the place at each canton where the popular meetings must be held.

No. 21.

Provisions of the Decree of Bases and Guarantees of March 8, 1841, in regard to Costa Rican Territory.

ARTICLE I.

Of the State.

§ 1. The State consists of all its inhabitants whether native or naturalized. It is sovereign and independent both in its internal administration and its foreign relations. The sovereignty essentially resides in the whole of the State; and no section thereof, whether large or small, nor any person exercising the supreme power, shall assume the title of sovereign.

§ 2. THE TERRITORY OF THE STATE IS COMPRISED WITHIN THE FOLLOWING LIMITS: ON THE WEST THE LA FLOR RIVER, AND THE CONTINUATION OF THE LINE THEREOF, AND ALONG THE SHORE OF THE LAKE OF NICARAGUA AND THE SAN JUAN RIVER TO THE MOUTH OF THE LATTER ON THE ATLANTIC; ON THE NORTH THE ATLANTIC OCEAN FROM THE MOUTH OF THE SAN JUAN RIVER TO THE ESCUDO DE VERAGUA; on the east from the latter place to the Chiriquí river; AND ON THE SOUTH FROM THE LATTER RIVER AND ALL ALONG THE COAST OF THE PACIFIC OCEAN TO THE LA FLOR RIVER.

§ 3. The territory of the State is divided into five Departments, the capitals of which shall be, respectively, Cartago, San José, Heredia, Alajuela, and GUANACASTE. The first will consist of all the towns between Matina and the El Fierro river; the second will be comprised between the latter river and the Virilla river, including the towns of Térraba and Boruca. The third department will be comprised between the Virilla and the Segundo rivers. The fourth will be comprised between the Segundo and the Chomes rivers; and the FIFTH WILL BE COMPRISED BETWEEN THE CHOMES AND THE LA FLOR RIVERS. The Departments are subdivided into towns, and the towns into wards and sections, but the titles so far obtained of cities and towns shall be preserved ; but in the future no such titles shall be granted, except for great services rendered to the State. When the increase of the population may demand another distribution of the Departments, all new arrangements shall be based upon the rate of 30,000 inhabitants for each one.

No. 22.

The Constituent Assembly of Costa Rica of 1842 declared that the Province of Guanacaste is an integral part of the national territory and that it is incumbent upon the honor of the nation to repel the aggression attempted by Nicaragua.

The Provisional Supreme Chief Magistrate of the State of Costa Rica,

Whereas the Constituent Assembly has decreed what follows :

The Constituent Assembly of the State of Costa Rica, upon consideration of the decree enacted by the Legislative Assembly of the State of Nicaragua, dated May 24th instant, giving authority to the Supreme Director of that State to actually annex to it the District of Guanacaste ; and considering :

1st. That by decree of the Federal Congress of December 9, 1825, THE SAID DEPARTMENT WAS INCORPORATED INTO THE TERRITORY of Costa Rica, until the demarcation of the States provided for by Article VII of the Constitution of the Republic was accomplished.

2d. That by virtue of the said decree THE STATE TOOK POSSESSION OF THE SAID DEPARTMENT AND ADMINISTERED THE GOVERNMENT THEREOF, with just title, and has retained it ever since AS AN INTEGRAL PART OF ITS TERRITORY.

3d. That ever since the emancipation from the Spanish Government, the local and municipal authorities of those towns and villages have always shown their decided desire that Guanacaste should BE ANNEXED TO THE TERRITORY OF COSTA RICA, repeated applications having been made by them to that effect, as witnessed by the preliminary remarks of the aforesaid decree of December 9th.

4th. That subsequently to the disruption of the national representation in 1838, the people of that locality, through their respective authorities, SOLEMNLY REITERATED THEIR DECISION to continue united to Costa Rica.

5th. That THE REINCORPORATION OF THAT DEPARTMENT TO NICARAGUA, AS IS ATTEMPTED, is an usurpation of the indisputable right to possess it given by law to Costa Rica, and that in consequence it is incumbent upon the honor and the duty of the State TO PRESERVE THE INTEGRITY OF ITS TERRITORY and the dignity of its name, repelling by all means the aggression which is intended against it for the purpose of despoiling it of its property.

By unanimous vote decrees:

ARTICLE I. THE DEPARTMENT OF GUANACASTE IS AN INTEGRAL PART OF THE TERRITORY OF COSTA RICA.

ARTICLE II. The Executive shall see by all means that THE INTEGRITY OF THE STATE, its dignity and its rights shall be preserved.

Let it be communicated to the Executive for due execution and in order that it may be printed, published and circulated.

Given at the City of San José on the 25th day of August, 1842.

JOSÉ FRANCISCO PERALTA,
President.

JOAQUIN B. CALVO,
Secretary.

FELIX SANCHO,
Secretary.

Therefore let it be executed, circulated, and published.
Government House, San José, August 27, 1842.

FRANCISCO MORAZÁN.

To General JOSÉ MIGUEL SARAVIA.

No. 23.

Revenue posts are established on the Sarapiqui and La Flor rivers.

The President of the State of Costa Rica,

Upon information that foreign goods, as well as those articles the traffic of which the Government has reserved for itself, are frequently smuggled into this State through the northern coast, the Sarapiquí river, and the western frontier ; and considering that it is the duty of the Executive to prevent this trade from being carried on, to the detriment both of lawful commerce and the public Treasury ; in use of the faculties vested in him by sections 22 and 26 of Article 110 of the Constitution, and by the law of December 31, 1845, decrees :

ARTICLE I. A revenue military post is established on the northern coast, on the banks of the SARAPIQUÍ river ; and another of the same kind upon the BANKS OF THE LA FLOR RIVER,[1] in the western part of the State ; and both of them will be stationed at the places which the Government may designate.

ARTICLE II. Each one of these posts will be in charge of a commandant, subject to the orders of the Intendente-General ; and this commander shall have under him such troops as according to the circumstances may be determined.

ARTICLE III. It will be the duty of those posts to seize the merchandise and goods unlawfully introduced into the State, and also to prevent all persons from going out of the State without exhibiting their proper passports ; and after six months subsequent to the date of this decree it shall be also their duty to take to the interior any person who does not come provided with that document.

ARTICLE IV. The said posts shall be entitled to that share

------

[1] This was the boundary of Costa Rica after the annexation of Guanacaste.

of the articles seized which is allowed by law in recompense of this service.

Given at the city of San José, on May 10, 1847.

JOSÉ MARIA CASTRO.

To Señor Juan de Dios Zéspedes,
  Chief of Bureau, in charge pro tem.
    of the Departments of War and Treasury.

No. 24.

The Congress of Costa Rica approves the Executive Decree which establishes military revenue posts on the Sarapiqui river and the western frontier of Nicaragua.

DEPARTMENT OF THE TREASURY, WAR, AND NAVY.

No. 266.- Circular.

GOVERNMENT HOUSE,
SAN JOSÉ, *June* 16, 1847.

The Constitutional Congress communicated to me on the 11th instant what follows:

" The Constitutional Congress having taken into consideration the communication made by the Executive on the 27th of May ultimo, asking for the approval of Decree No. 1, dated on the 10th of the same month, by which two military revenue posts are established on the Nicaraguan frontier, and on the banks of the Sarapiqui river; and taking into consideration the provisions of § 26 of Article 110 of the fundamental law, and the report of the proper committee, has been pleased, at a meeting held yesterday, to approve said Decree. And I have the honor to transmit it to you by order of the President of this State, for your information and the proper effect, hoping that you will be pleased to acknowledge the receipt of this communication, and to accept the consideration with which I subscribe myself your obedient servant.

By the Minister :

JUAN DE DIOS ZÉSPEDEZ,
Chief of Bureau.

No. 25.

The road which leads to the La Flor river, the frontier of the States of Costa Rica and Nicaragua, is ordered to be repaired.

JUAN RAFAEL MORA, President of the Republic of Costa Rica:

Whereas the Constitutional Congress has decreed as follows:

The Constitutional Congress of the Republic of Costa Rica, taking into consideration that the tax of one-half real (6¼ cents), levied at the toll-gate upon each head of cattle passing through there, was created by the law of August 7, 1827, to be used in part for the opening and repair of the road leading to the frontiers of the State of Nicaragua, which object has not been realized; and also considering that the residents and land-owners of the Province of Guanacaste, upon whom the said tax was especially laid, demand that this money be used for the aforesaid purposes; and considering that it is of the highest importance to the commerce and industry of the country, that the means of communication between this Republic and the neighboring State should be facilitated, has been pleased to decree, and decrees:

ARTICLE I. Out of the amount realized from the tax imposed upon cattle by the law of August 7, 1847, there shall be placed at the disposition of the Governor of the Province of Guanacaste the sum of $500, to be used in the opening of the road which leads from the BARRANCA TO THE LA FLOR river,[1] the said tax being devoted in the future to the repair and improvement of the said road.

To the Executive Power.

---

[1] Boundary of the two States at the date of this decree.

Given at the Palace of the Supreme Powers in San José, on the 11th day of July, 1851.

FRANCISCO MARIA OREAMUNO,
President.

MODESTO GUEVARA,
Secretary.

MIGUEL MORA,
Secretary.

Therefore let it be executed.

National Palace, San José, July 28, 1851.

JUAN RAFAEL MORA.
MANUEL JOSÉ CARAZO.

To The Secretary of War and of the Treasury.

No. 26.

Bases for the formation of a Company, named the Sarapiqui Company, for the opening of a road from San José to the Sarapiqui river, and for the navigation of the said river, in order that the exportations of Costa Rica may be made through the San Juan river.

JUAN RAFAEL MORA, President of the Republic of Costa Rica:

Taking into consideration:

1st. that the prosperity of the country being based upon agriculture and commerce, it is of the highest importance to improve those two great fountains of wealth in order that they may improve day by day and reach perfection.

2d. That one of the best means of reaching the end indicated is to lay out convenient and short roads leading to the ports on both oceans.

3d. That at present the Republic owns a very good road on the Pacific that can be improved; and that there is none on the side of the Atlantic, although such a one has been demanded for a long time by the urgent interest of the Costa Rican people.

4th. That several schemes, surveys, and examinations have been undertaken FOR THE LAST 30 YEARS AT DIFFERENT TIMES by several citizens of the nation in order to accomplish such a desired purpose.

5th. That subsequently to the said attempts the discovery was made of the means of building a road giving easy access to the SARAPIQUÍ RIVER, WHICH IS NAVIGABLE, AND EMPTIES INTO THE SAN JUAN RIVER, WHICH IN ITS TURN EMPTIES INTO THE NORTHERN SEA, where there is a good port known and frequented by all commercial nations.

6th. That the Government, yielding to the general clamor, and taking advantage of that discovery, gave the proper authority, for a formal survey, and for the BUILDING OF THE ROAD, and appropriated for that purpose a portion of the revenue devoted to roads; and that the said formal survey proved to be successful, and also that the work began, but could not be completed, for want of means.

7th. That if the necessity of such an easy way of communication to the Atlantic has heretofore been imperious, now it is still more urgent, owing to the increase of the population and industry of the country, as shown by statistics.

8th. And, finally, that the frequency of relations of this country with foreign States, is conducive to immense benefit for its wealth and civilization, and anticipates a great and flattering future for the Republic, I have been pleased to decree, and do hereby decree, as follows:

ARTICLE I. Due authority is given for the organization in this country of a Costa Rican Company, to be known as the Sarapiqui Company, consisting of twenty responsible members, and having a capital of $60,000, divided into shares of $3,000 for each partner: the said capital to be increased hereafter, if necessary.

ARTICLE II. This company shall have for its object the building of a substantial carriage road, within the period of five years, to be counted from January 1, 1852, starting from this city, and ending on the wharf of the Sarapiqui river. The width of this road shall be 40 yards, whenever the topographic conditions of the locality permits it; and it shall be provided with such bridges and other appurtenances as are necessary for its use and preservation.

ARTICLE III. Notwithstanding the provisions of the preceding Article, the company shall begin by building, as soon as possible, a good road for mules, which shall be finished within eighteen months, to be counted from the same day, January 1, 1852.

ARTICLE IX. It is hereby granted in favor of the said Company that it shall collect during the period of twenty-five years toll tax of two reals (25 cents) for each one hundred-weight of all domestic merchandise that may be carried over the whole of the said road, or a part thereof, and four reals

(50 cents) for each one hundredweight of foreign merchandise, of whatever nature, imported through it.

ARTICLE XVIII. The Company shall have the right for the period of five years of establishing, if suitable to its interests, STEAM NAVIGATION ON THE SARAPIQUÍ RIVER, either by itself or by agreement with other companies; and, in either event, the Government grants to it, for the whole period of the contract for the road, the right to collect a navigation duty of one real (12½ cents) on each one hundredweight of merchandise exported, and two reals (25 cents) for each one hundredweight of merchandise imported.

Given at the National Palace, at San José, on October 27, 1851.

JUAN RAFAEL MORA.
JOAQUIN BERNARDO CALVO,
Secretary of the Interior.

No. 27.

Costa Rica prohibits the Navigation of the San Cárlos river, an affluent of the San Juan, and prescribes penalties for the transgressors.

JUAN RAFAEL MORA, President of the Republic of Costa Rica:

Whereas I have been informed that foreign merchandise, and also those articles, the trade of which the Government has reserved for itself, are frequently smuggled through the San Cárlos river, therefore I do hereby decree-

ARTICLE 1. NAVIGATION ON THE SAN CÁRLOS RIVER IS HEREBY PROHIBITED, until said river is declared, with the proper formalities, to be a port of the Republic.

ARTICLE 2. Every boat or vessel which may be found NAVIGATING ON THE SAN CÁRLOS RIVER shall be seized and forfeited, together with everything on board, whether it is foreign merchandise, or not; and the owner, or master, and the sailors thereof, shall be arrested and placed at the disposal of the judge of the Treasury, to be tried according to law.

ARTICLE 3. A PERAMBULATING REVENUE POST subordinate to the Rio Grande Custom House, and consisting of one corporal and three revenue guards, is hereby established, and it shall be its duty to watch over the roads leading to the San Cárlos river, and GUARD THE BANKS OF THE SAME.

ARTICLE 4. Such foreign merchandise, or articles whose trade belongs to the Government, as may be seized by this revenue post, shall be delivered, together with the prisoner, or prisoners, to the Collector of the Custom House above-named, and said collector shall distribute the captured property, according to the laws and decrees in force.

Given at the Palace of the Government in San José, on November 14, 1853.

JUAN RAFAEL MORA.
MANUEL JOSÉ CARAZO,
Secretary of the Treasury.

No. 28.

Costa Rica grants to the firm of Kirkland & Geering the privilege of steam navigation on the Sapoá river, and of establishing a route of transit from the Bolaños Bay to the Lake of Nicaragua; the grantees being authorized to use the waters of the Lake and of the San Juan and Colorado rivers, in so far as they belong to Costa Rica.

Juan Rafael Mora, the President of the Republic of Costa Rica:

Whereas the Constitutional Congress has decreed as follows:

The Constitutional Congress of the Republic of Costa Rica, upon examination of the contract entered into on February 25th instant, between the Government of the Republic and Messrs. William P. Kirkland, William B. Geering, and their associates for the purpose of establishing a line of transit BE-TWEEN THE PORT OF LAS SALINAS DE BOLAÑOS TO THE SAPOÁ RIVER AND Port of San Juan, has been pleased to decree, and decrees:

ARTICLE 1. The contract of February 25th instant, between the Republic and William P. Kirkland, William B. Geering, and their associates is hereby approved with the amendments set forth in the following article:

ARTICLE II. The amendments spoken of in the foregoing Article are the following:

1st. The Article of the contract will read as follows:

" The Government of Costa Rica grants to Messrs. William P. Kirkland, William B. Geering, and their associates, the exclusive privilege of STEAM NAVIGATION ON THE SAPOÁ RIVER for the purpose of establishing a line of transit FROM THE GULF OF LAS SALINAS DE BOLAÑOS TO THE LAKE OF NICARAGUA, for the period of twenty years, to be counted from the date of this decree; and the said Messrs. William P. Kirkland, William B. Geering, and their associates, are hereby declared to form a corporation, or partnership, or company, which shall be known from this date by the name of TRANSIT COMPANY OF

COSTA RICA. In order to carry this undertaking into effect the said Company SHALL HAVE THE POWER TO USE FREELY THE WATERS OF THE LAKE OF NICARAGUA[1] AND THE SAN JUAN AND COLORADO RIVERS IN THE PART THEREOF WHICH BELONGS TO SAID REPUBLIC OF COSTA RICA."

2d. The new road shall not impede the free travel of the other Republics of Central America which has been permitted by this Republic.

3d. Article 10 of the above mentioned contract shall be understood as follows: The employees and laborers of the Company, whilst they remain such, shall be free from all civil and military service; but in urgent cases they shall render such services as the Government may require.

4th. An additional article shall be inserted in the above-named contract, in the following terms:

" If within six months from this date the Company should not have commenced the works which the enterprise requires, and if the transit should not be established within eighteen months, the said contract shall become null and of no effect, and the Republic shall be at full liberty to dispose, as it may deem convenient, of the favors granted to said Company."

To the Executive Power.

Given in the Hall Sessions in San José, the 22d day of May, 1854.

FRANCISCO MARIA OREAMUNO,
President.

MODESTO GUEVARA,
Secretary.

JESUS JIMENEZ,
Secretary.

Therefore let it be executed.

National Palace, San José, May 23, 1854.

JUAN RAFAEL MORA.

JOAQUIN BERNARDO CALVO,
Secretary of the Interior.

_____

[1] It will be rembered that Costa Rica before the treaty of 1858 was a border State of the Lake of Nicaragua.

No. 29.

The Government of Costa Rica accepts the apology made by the Government of Nicaragua for having trespassed with its forces upon the dividing line between the two States, that is, the La Flor river, boundary of the Costa Rican Province of Guanacaste.

SAN JOSÉ, *September* 3, 1855.

To the Minister of Foreign Relations of the Supreme Government of the Republic of Nicaragua.

SIR: I received yesterday at 12 M. your estimable note, No. 13. in reply to the one which I had the honor to address to you on July 23d last.

It would not be difficult for me to answer to every one of your able arguments, or prove satisfactorily, that my Government, taking into consideration the information at that time received, justly felt itself wounded in what is most sacred to a free people, which is national honor and sovereignty, and was right in demanding from your Government a public apology and the punishment of the invaders. But the statement made through you by your Government conveys such a full, frank, and sincere explanation of all the facts which alarmed us, as to prove that there has not been any desire or intention of offending the people and Government of Costa Rica.

In reading the statements therein made by your enlightened Government, under your authorized signature, that neither the Executive of Nicaragua, nor its subordinate authorities, ever had any intention to cause the slightest displeasure to the Government and people of Costa Rica, with which it desires to cultivate relations of fraternity and harmony, I cannot but be persuaded of the sincerity with which your Government, wisely laying aside the delicate question of principle, deemed it preferable to justify itself by claiming to have acted upon sentiments of fraternity and common interest, and by urging its acts to have been accomplished with good intention under the pressure of circumstances, and not looking at Costa Rica as a foreign nation, but as a friend and a sister.

And above all, my Government being anxious that it may never be supposed that Costa Rica, taking advantage of the domestic troubles which embarrass your unfortunate country, and of the civil war and the epidemics which horribly devour its children, wishes to increase its misfortunes and render its unfortunate situation graver, by insisting upon her demands, I have now the great pleasure to answer to you that my Government, setting aside said demands, and seeing in the two nations nothing else than members of the same family, which must keep cordially united to each other in fraternal relations, declares itself satisfied with the very attentive, conciliatory, and well-supported explanation, which you have given on behalf of your Government.

I have been deeply impressed by that paragraph of your note in which you feelingly say: "The foreign enemy, Sir, is threatening us; the danger is imminent; *and before that danger, it is necessary for us all to repress any complaint, no matter how just,* desist from family quarrels, and set aside all questions."

These are beautiful and well-expressed sentiments, the frequent repetition of which renders it, however, difficult to understand, how it is that they are not carried into practice in the terrible struggle which afflicts Nicaragua.

You know well that the constant current of our thought has run in that direction ; that in the midst of our peace and prosperity we, Costa Ricans, never forget that we all are Central-Americans ; but I shall not fail to say that your sympathetic and correct remarks have powerfully impressed the noble mind of his Excellency the President and hastened the oblivion of the events which caused on him such a deep impression. The President trusts that in the future there will never be any disagreement between the two countries, nor will anything interrupt the happy harmony which to-day more than ever must unite, not only the two Republics, but all the Central-American States.

I shall not end this communication without assuring you that each and all the acts done by order of my Government, and of which you make a detailed enumeration, have been prompted only by the full conviction of our rights; but, as there seems to be some doubt about its legality on the part of your Government, we are ready to adjust the matters peacefully as is proper among sister nations.

Now, more than on any other occasion, it is gratifying to me to offer to you my respects as your most obedient servant and friend,

J. BERNARDO CALVO.

["Boletin Oficial," 2d year, No. 126. San Jose, September, 12, 1885].

No. 30.

Congratulation of the people of Leon to the Costa Rican Army upon the seizure of the steamers and its control of the river and Lake.

To the Costa Rican Soldiers :

The people of Leon open their arms to you in token of their eternal gratitude for your heroic efforts in saving Nicaragua and the whole of Central America from vandalism, and in liber_ating them from the clutches of William Walker, the worse of tyrants, who had no other object in view than war, bloodshed, destruction, and absolute ruin of every town and city through which he might pass, and who, in his fury, never respects even the Temples of God.

Providence has placed in your hands, as can be seen, the sword which has to exterminate that infernal dragon, whenever he presents himself. You shall conquer him ; you shall drive him from the soil of your forefathers, overwhelmed with confusion, and recognizing that Central America is not an uncivilized country as he has said, and that it prefers death to degradation and infamy.

We congratulate you, and congratulate ourselves, for the brilliant triumph achieved by you in reconquering the Lake and the San Juan river, and in causing the enemy to sustain such immense losses; and you may rest assured that we on our part shall co-operate with pleasure in all your efforts, since we are certain that God guides your steps and leads you in recognition of your *holy intentions* (santas intenciones) through the path of glory.

Leon, January 10th, 1857.

THE PEOPLE OF LEON.

[From the "Boletin Oficial" of Leon, transcribed in the "Boletin Oficial" of Costa Rica, No. 265, February 11th, 1857].

No. 31.

Seizure of the steamers of the San Juan river and the Lake of Nicaragua.—Official news from the Army.—Another triumph.—Go ahead!—The war nearly at an end.

The information received to-day from the San Juan river and transmitted by Gen. Don José Joaquin Mora is very satisfactory.

On December 28th our troops seized the two steamers at the Rapids of El Toro and Machuca, captured the fortress of Castillo Viejo, which is on the river bank, and also took possession of the steamer Virgen, which was well armed and loaded with cannons, rifles, gunpowder, swords, &c., &c., to the value of more than ten thousand dollars.

The steamer Virgen had been Walker's most powerful auxiliary. With it he ran over the waters of the river and Lake, and, safely and without opposition, made repeated attacks wherever he pleased, taking advantage of the helpless condition of the allies, who, lacking vessels, saw themselves compelled to operate on land by fatiguing and protracted marches.

The enemy does not count any more upon the powerful assistance on which it has relied to escape so many attacks, and move rapidly from one place to another according to his wishes.

Our troops have now seven steamers on the Lake and on the San Juan river.

The important strategic points of La Trinidad and Castillo Viejo on the river are well guarded, their fortifications have been improved, their garrisons have been reinforced, and everything will be done immediately to preserve them in a perfect condition of safety and defence.

General Mora, preceded by a gallant division, was marching to attack the San Cárlos fortress on the Lake shore.

The only steamer left to the bandit Walker, which is the one named "San Cárlos," seriousl damaged by Central-American shot, must by this time be in our hands.

Our army, therefore, is in full possession of the Lake, and can freely communicate with General Cañas and the commanding officers of the allied armies at Granada, Masaya, and neighboring places.

Such successful operations have not required the sacrifice of any lives. Courage, boldness, and the surprises given the enemies secured the triumph.

The allied armies, united and well organized, were at the end of last week preparing themselves to march against Walker.

Desertion was increasing among the filibusters; and hunger as well as fever demoralizes them and compels them to remain in deadly inaction.

God visibly protects our cause, and will grant us very soon a complete victory.

[Extracts from the official report of General Mora].

No. 32.

Proclamation of the President of Costa Rica upon the seizure of the steamers and the control of the San Juan river and the Lake of Nicaragua.

OFFICIAL.

The President of the Republic to the People of Costa Rica.

FELLOW-CITIZENS: The great artery of filibusterism has been severed forever. The sword of Costa Rica has cut it.

In twenty days of campaign, through deserts full of vipers, through thick forests, through terrible marshes and swamps, through large rivers, our soldiers have marched with the step of conquerors, and taken possession of La Trinidad, Castillo Viejo, the San Cárlos fortress, eight steamers and some other boats, ten pieces of cannon, three mortars, five hundred rifles, a great number of swords, revolvers, and all kinds of ammunition of war, and more than one hundred enemies whom we have generously released. Now, upon the waters of the San Juan river and of the Great Lake, the rays of the sun do not shine upon any other flag than that of Costa Rica.

All has been conquered without one shot, without a drop of blood, by intrepidity and surprise. And what were our means of action? The fleet with which we attacked the steamers of our strong enemies were trunks of trees scarcely hewed out, or badly bound with vines. The muskets which we had in our hands were rusty, and could hardly be used on account of their continual exposure to rain. We had no provisions. We had nothing. But we had courage, self-denial, patriotism, that union of mind peculiar to Costa Rica, and the decision to conquer or to die. And Providence has blessed our soldiers, and conducted them from victory to victory.

We are masters of the river and the Great Lake, and are in communication with our allies, while Walker, who is confined to Rivas and its neighboring territory, is going to be attacked and conquered and annihilated, together with the city, if such is necessary. I have offered pardon to all those who blindly follow him, if they should abandon his cause. We shall know how to conquer and forgive.

But will this be the end ? No, fellow-citizens. The work commenced must be terminated. It is necessary for us not to be subject any more to the danger that a new Walker comes to disturb our peace, and struggle to reduce us to slavery. It is necessary that so many obstacles overcome, so many sacrifices made, shall not become fruitless. They have to be continued. Let us, therefore, raise upon that very river, and with our own hands, a powerful barrier which may now and forever stop that torrent of usurpation. Nothing would have been gained by only obtaining a precarious peace. Let us conquer a solid, lasting peace, honorable, and producive of fruitful results to Costa Rica, Nicaragua, and the Central American States.

Costa Ricans, I rely upon you for all of this. With your assistance and Divine protection, there will be nothing to stop me. Let us bless Providence which shelters us, and let us march united, at the cry of Long live Costa Rica ! with undisturbed faith and perseverance towards the future which is before us.

JUAN R. MORA.

San José, *January* 11, 1857.

No. 33.

Opinion of the Government of Guatemala in regard to the action of Costa Rica during the war against Walker, and especially in the affair of the seizure of the steamers.

Costa Rica has again gallantly undertaken a campaign against the invaders of Nicaragua. She understood the importance of occupying certain places on the San Juan river to prevent the adventurers from being reinforced by way of the Northern Sea, and her troops have succeeded in accomplishing this purpose by seizing the steamers which Walker had on the river, occupying the San Cárlos fortress, which is upon the very same entrance to the Lake, and by taking possession also, as is said, of one of the two steamers that the enemy had on the Lake. * * *

It is certainly sad, and causes the soul of any person who is friendly to the independence of the country to grieve, that while Costa Rica is making new and strenuous efforts to save Nic_aragua, and while the other Central American Republics are preparing themselves to send troops to replace the losses sustained in their ranks, there seems to be nothing, even the imminence of danger, capable of terminating the unhappy discord which has brought unfortunate Nicaragua to the condition in which she now finds herself.

["Gaceta de Guatemala," January 22, 1857.]

No. 34.

*What happened in Nicaragua after the seizure of the steamers
by the Costa Rican forces.*

San José, *February* 4, 1857.

News from the Army.

[Extracts from official despatches and documents].

After twenty days of silence and anxiety, we have at last
received the news from the army which we published in the
extra editions of the "Boletin" issued on the 2d and 3d
instant.

What is the reason of such great calm, of such an incompre-
hensible inaction, before an enemy who, although conquered,
is so active, astute, and bold?

We do not believe in concealing the truth, but, on the contrary, in proclaiming it aloud, and making it serve us as an example, to avoid disunion and internal discord, which inevitably
produce the ruin of all nations. Nicaragua is unfortunately
the living, bloody, smoky, example, which Costa Rica must
have before her eyes to confirm her in her love of peace, and
of her modest and industrious existence, free from the accursed
rancor of parties, and to make her preserve, above all things,
the most vigorous union among her children.

The field of the Central American allies has been about to
offer the image of another "Agramante's field." Partisan
spirit, lamentable preferences, repeated disagreements, and lastly
a fatal division, caused the armies, already decimated by sickness and war, to be disbanded. When Gen. Cañas arrived[1]
there, he did all that he could to re-establish indispensable unity
among the leaders and the troops; and considering the state of
irritation, and the almost irreconcilable differences which he

---

[1] Gen. Don José Maria Cañas, a Costa Rican officer, who afterwards gave
his name to the treaty of 1858.

found there, what he succeeded in accomplishing cannot be deemed small.

The triumphs obtained by Costa Rica on the San Juan river caused a reanimation of the spirits of Nicaragua, the concentration of her thoughts, the oblivion of her petty differences, and the prevalence of the noble idea of saving the country from traitorous and foreign enemies.

As soon as General Mora[1] reached the fortress of San Cárlos, he devoted himself with characteristic activity, as well as decision and tact, to accomplish a powerful harmonization of all conflicting elements, and by calling together the Central American leaders, and writing to the Generals of the armies, and to every one who could exercise any influence in that direction, he prepared the way to give the *coup de grace* to the usurpers.

All of this has fortunately succeeded. All the leaders have responded with patriotism and dignity to the appeal of the Costa Rican Generals, who, being exempted from partisan spirit, have no other feeling than the desire to fulfil their duty towards their common country, and to fortify the Central American independence by expelling from the Central American soil the last one of its enemies.

Under such circumstances nothing exists now which prevents military operations from being carried on; and it may be that, at the time of writing this, a terrible end has been reached by the enemy to the benefit and prosperity of Central America.

---

[1] Don José Joaquin Mora, a brother of Don Juan Rafael Mora, President of Costa Rica.

No. 35.

What, in 1857, was thought in Nicaragua in regard to the blow inflicted by Costa Rica upon Walker on the San Juan river and the Lake of Nicaragua.

[From the " Boletin Oficial" of Leon.]

The Vanguard of Central America.

Three hundred years ago a clever Minister of the English Government, placing his finger upon the map of the New World, recently discovered, pointed at the Isthmus of Nicaragua as the great door through which Europe should place herself in rapid communication with China, Japan, and the Indian Archipelago. At the end of last century a Spanish Minister saw in the same Isthmus the proper place for the opening of an interoceanic canal; and at the beginning of the present century a scientific commission of the Spanish Government made the proper surveys. Lately, on September 22, 1849, and August 19, 1851, a passage from San Juan del Sur, the Lake, and the river of San Juan del Norte, until the port of the same name on the Atlantic was successfully made ; and the door was thrown open through which our independence can be threatened at any moment, as it has been now threatened, with the knowledge and acquiescence of the nation which seems to show the greatest interest for the non-alienation of the said transit. The Republic of Costa Rica, surrounded by the waters and territory of Nicaragua on her northern side, from east to west, finds herself much more in contact with the said line than all the other States, and it is for this reason that she is called by nature to be the sentry and the " Vanguard of Central America."

Costa Rica, indeed, has understood very well her own mission in the present struggle against the filibusters ; she was the first to take the field on April 11 last, and defeated the enemy, rendering it incapable to follow the rapid march which it intended. She could then measure the strength of the enemy, and, casting her inquiring look upon the battle-field, she saw through the smoke of gunpowder and the noise of the struggle, that the vital point of Walker laid on the extremity of the transit line, as the strength of Sampson was in his hair. At once, and without hesitating one single moment, she left Rivas to engage in new strategic operations which she carried on with great success by marching her victorious armies from the San Cárlos river to Punta de Castilla in the port of San Juan del Norte, and from Castillo Viejo to the fort and Lake of Nicaragua, depriving filibusters of their steamers, their rifles, their cannons, their ammunition of war, and closing the door through which they could escape or receive reinforcements. All of this was done while the allied forces, abandoning Rivas to the enemy, compelled the invaders to concentrate themselves in a small place without any possibility to pay attention to the movements of that formidable vanguard.

Costa Rica, which scarcely has a population of 100,000 inhabitants, has put on the field more than 5,000 men. She has opened her treasures, free of cost, to all those who, whether through need or deceit, followed Walker. She has fitted out national men-of-war and chartered others which will very soon efficiently blockade the southern port; and in this way she has raised so high the national flag that it can be seen from every distance, and show that Costa Rica is indeed the Vanguard of Central America.

G. J.

No. 36.

*The public opinion of Nicaragua in regard to Costa Rica in
1857.—Nicaragua.—The United States of Costa Rica and
Nicaragua.*

This would be the name of the Republic formed by the
union of the two countries, and this is the destiny to which
they are called by their past, present, and future conditions.

If the States of Guatemala, Salvador, and Honduras were,
during the colonial rule, three entities actually different from
each other, Costa Rica and Nicaragua were considered as only
one Province, notwithstanding their nominal separation.

There was not between them an absolute independence.
Each had a Governor, but one of these governors was a sub-
delegate of the other. There was only one political chief, and
both Territories constituted but one diocese. The Costa Rican
people got from Nicaragua their wives, their learning, and
their fortune; and their children, Nicaraguans by nature, returned to Costa Rica to recognize the land of their parents
and strengthen still more the bonds of consanguinity, wealth,
and intelligence which connected them to each other. At
present both Republics need union as a means to preserve their
independence, dangerously compromised by the impetuous torrent of the immense commercial movement of the whole world,
carried from one ocean to the other through their respective
territories.

Union alone can make them strong enough to oppose this
inevitable movement. Only a condition of union in which all
their interests are founded may render them respectable, and
only in this way they will be able to cultivate the science of
foreign politics with advantages that cannot be found under a
separate system.

No. 37.

Gratuitous grant of lands along the course of the Sarapiqui river down to its confluence with the San Juan river, for agricultural purposes.

RAFAEL G. ESCALANTE,
 *Vice-President of the Republic of Costa Rica, acting
 as Supreme Chief Executive Magistrate of the same:*

Moved by the desire of favoring the poor people of Costa Rica by granting them gratuitously such tracts of lands as are capable of giving support to their families, and having in view at the same time the advisability of promoting and facilitating foreign immigration by making grants of the lands more fertile and better situated for commerce, I do hereby decree:

ARTICLE 1. A strip of vacant land 500 yards wide is appropriated on the TWO BANKS OF THE SARAPIQUÍ RIVER, AND ALL ALONG ITS COURSE UNTIL ITS CONFLUENCE WITH THE SAN JUAN RIVER, for the exclusive purpose of being given to poor Costa Ricans and to the industrious people of any nationality who may be willing to settle there and cultivate the land under the rules established by this decree.

ARTICLE 2. Each settler shall be given a square area embracing five manzanas, or 50,000 square yards, with a river front of 100 yards and a depth of 500; and between one piece of property and the other, a street 20 yards wide shall be left, in order to facilitate the access to the other vacant grounds beyond the limits of this strip.

ARTICLE 3. All those who shall settle within two years from this date shall enjoy the favors herein granted; but those who shall not cultivate their lands within five years, also to be counted from this date, shall forfeit their right in the land.

ARTICLE 4. The grantee who shall have complied with the conditions of the foregoing Article, besides enjoying the favors aforesaid, shall be entitled to an addittional square area, equal in extent to the one cultivated by him, in order that he may use it as he deems best; but it shall be located in the rear of the cultivated lot.

ARTICLE 5. If the settler should be willing to engage himself, in addition to the purposes spoken of in the preceding article, in cultivating cocoa, and shall have raised a cocoa plantation within the five years spoken of in Article 3, he shall be entitled to the ownership of the ground which he has devoted to that cultivation, provided that it is distant at least one thousand yards from the banks of the Sarapiquí river.

ARTICLE 6. All foreigners who shall desire to avail themselves of the opportunities of the present decree may either directly apply to the Judge of the Treasury or send his application through the COMMANDANT OF SARAPIQUÍ, setting forth his intention of becoming a Costa Rican citizen, and asking to be given possession of the land which he must first cultivate. The Judge of the Treasury will direct the Commandant of Sarapiquí to give the possession asked for, and will enter into the proper register, which the said judge shall keep, the name, sex, age, profession or trade, condition, and nationality of the settler.

ARTICLE 7. If the settler is a Costa Rican citizen he shall also file before the Judge of the Treasury a certificate of the Governor of the Province where he lives, showing that this decree is applicable to him on account of his poverty, and the said judge shall direct upon inspection of the said certificate that the COMMANDANT OF SARAPIQUÍ should give him possession of the area marked by law, the proper register being previously made as aforesaid.

ARTICLE 8. As soon as the Commandant of Sarapiquí gives the settler the possession of the land which he intends to cultivate and which was selected by him, he shall issue a certificate witnessing the fact and clearly designating the location of the area to which it refers. This certificate shall be sufficient title for the settler for the purpose of asking both the survey and the ownership of the land to which he may be entitled; but it shall be of no use to him if he has not complied with the conditions above established within the time provided for.

ARTICLE 9. After the expiration of the 5 years prescribed by this decree, or before if the conditions have been fulfiled, the settlers shall apply to the Judge of the Treasury, setting forth the favors which he has deserved, and asking for a title of ownership.

ARTICLE 10. The Judge of the Treasury, upon examination of three witnesses testifying that the petitioner has complied with the required conditions, shall declare him entitled to the favor or favors herein granted, and shall transmit the record of the case to the Government in order that the patent or title shall be issued.

ARTICLE 11. Both in the court of the Treasury, and in the office of the Commandant of Sarapiqui, all the fees to be charged in relation to these cases shall be reduced one-half. And the certificates and testimony received in support thereof, in relation to the said matter, shall be written on unstamped paper.

Given at the National Palace at San José on April 23, 1858.

RAFAEL G. ESCALANTE.

JOSÉ MARIA CAÑAS,
Secretary of the Treasury.

No. 38.

Provisions of the Nicaraguan Constitution of August 19, 1858, *in regard to limits and the division of the National territory.*

In the presence of God.

We, the representatives of the State, fully and legally authorized by our constituents to reform the Constitution of November 12, 1858, decree and sanction the following Political Constitution:

CHAPTER I.

Of the Republic.

ARTICLE 1. The Republic of Nicaragua is the same that was anciently called *Province*, and after the independence *State* of Nicaragua. Its territory is bounded on the east and northeast by the Sea of the Antilles; on the north and northwest by the State of Honduras; on the west and south by the Pacific Ocean; and on the southeast by the Republic of Costa Rica. THE LAWS UPON SPECIAL LIMITS FORM A PART OF THE CONSTITUTION.[1]

ARTICLE 3. THE TERRITORY SHALL BE DIVIDED for the different purposes of public administration into the departments, districts, and sections which the Constitution and laws shall provide for.[2]

*　　*　　*　　*　　*　　*　　*

[1] A few months before, the treaty of limits between Nicaragua and Costa Rica had been signed, ratified, exchanged, and approved, and this is the law evidently alluded to in this part of the new Constitution, since Nicaragua has no other law or treaty on limits.

[2] That law of territorial division was enacted by the same Constituent Assembly, and is Document No. 39 of this Appendix. In said territorial division the ancient district of Nicoya, was not, nor could it be, mentioned.

Given in the Hall of Sessions of the Constituent Assembly in Managua, the 19th day of August of the year of our Lord, 1858, and the 38th of our Independence.

HERMENEGILDO ZEPEDA,
Deputy for the District of Leon, President.

ANTONIO FALLA,
Deputy for the District of Rivas, Vice-President.

FELIX DE LA LLANA,
Deputy for the District of Leon.

CLETO MAYORGA,
Deputy for the District of Leon.

SANTIAGO PRADO,
Deputy for the District of Chinandega.

MARIANO RAMIREZ,
Deputy for the District of Chinandega.

HIPÓLITO GUTIERREZ,
Deputy for the District of Nueva Segovia.

PABLO CHAMORRO,
Deputy for the District of Matagalpa.

NARCISO ESPINOSA,
Deputy for the District of Matagalpa.

ISIDORO LOPEZ,
Deputy for the District of Masaya.

FRANCISCO JIMENEZ,
Deputy for the District of Granada.

JOSÉ L. CESAR,
Deputy for the District of Jinotepe.

J. MIGUEL CÁRDENAS,
Deputy for the District of Rivas.

E. CARAZO,
Deputy for the District of Rivas.

J. ARGÜELLO,
Deputy for the District of Rivas.

JOSE A. MEJIA,

Deputy for the District of Jinotepe.

J. MARIANO BOLÁNOS,

Deputy for the District of Masaya.[1]

MANAGUA, *August* 19, 1858.

Let it be executed.

Given under my hand and the seal of the Republic and countersigned by the Minister of Government.

TOMAS MARTINEZ.

ROSALIO CORTEZ,

Minister of Government.

---

[1] The districts represented by the Constituent Assembly were Leon, Rivas, Chinandega, Nueva Segovia, Matagalpa, Masaya, Granada, and Jinotepe. Nicoya was separated from Nicaragua since 1824.

No. 39.

Schedule of the Judicial Division of the territory of the Republic of Nicaragua.

DEPARTMENT OF GRANADA.

District of Granada.

Granada	Diriomo
Jinotepe	Diriá
Santa Teresa	San Juan
La Paz	Santa Catarina
El Rosario	Niquinohomo
Nandaimes	Diriamba

District of Masaya.

Masaya	Masatepe
Nindirí	San Marcos
Nandasmo	San Rafael

District of Managua.

Managua	Mateare
Tipitapa	

DEPARTMENT OF CHONTALES.

District of Acoyapa.

Acoyapa	Boaco
Lobago	San Lorenzo
Santo Tomás	Tenstepe
Juigalpa	San José
Comalapa	San Miguelito

District of San Cárlos.

San Cárlos.

District of Castillo Viejo.

Castillo Viejo.

District of San Juan del Norte.

San Juan del Norte.

DEPARTMENT OF CHINANDEGA.

District of Chinandega.

Chinandega	Posaltega
Viejo	Posalteguilla
Realejo	Somotillo
Chichigalpa	Villa Nueva
Guadalupe	

District of Corinto.

Corinto.

DEPARTMENT OF LEON.

District of Leon.

Leon	Telica
San Felipe	Quesalguaque
Subtiaba	Souse
Camoapa	

District of La Libertad.

Libertad.

DEPARTMENT OF NUEVA SEGOVIA

District of Nueva Segovia.

Somotogrande	Dipilto
Ocotal	Limay
Masonte	Estilí
Ciudad Antigua	Palacagüina
Jalapa	Jalagnina
Jicaro	Nagarote
Telpaneca	Pueblo Nuevo
Condega	Trinidad
Totogalpa	Pueblo Nuevo
Macualizo	San Buenaventura
Santa Maria	Santo Rosa

DEPARTMENT OF MATAGALPA.

District of Matagalpa.

Matagalpa	Tierra Bona
Jinotega	Esquipulas
San Rafael	Muimese
La Concordia	San Dionisio
Metopa	San Ramon
Sebace	

DEPARTMENT OF RIVAS.

District of Rivas.

Rivas	Ometepe
San Gorge	Moyogalpa
Buenos Ayres	Pineda
Potosi	La Virgen
Obrage	Tortuga

No. 40.

A road is ordered to be opened from the Capital to the Sarapiquí river.

JUAN RAFAEL MORA,
President of the Republic of Costa Rica.

Whereas the Congress has decreed the following :

The Constitutional Congress of the Republic of Costa Rica, having seen and examined the contract made on July 8th of the present year between the Supreme Government and the Messrs. Canty FOR THE PURPOSE OF BUILDING A ROAD FROM THIS CAPITAL TO THE SARAPIQUÍ RIVER, has been pleased to decree, and decrees :

SOLE ARTICLE. Let the 12 articles contained in the above-named contract be approved, as well as the additional article proposed by the Supreme Executive Power on July 9th of the present year, inserted in the same.

To the Supreme Executive Power.

Given in the Hall of Sessions, in San José, the 23d day of September, 1858.

RAFAEL G. ESCALANTE,
President.

JESUS JIMENEZ,
Secretary.

MANUEL CASTRO,
Secretary.

Therefore let it be executed.

National Palace, San José, September 27, 1858.

JUAN RAFAEL MORA.

JUAN BERNARDO CALVO,
Minister of the Interior and the Treasury.

No. 41.

Concessions made by Costa Rica for steam navigation upon the Sarapiquí and San Cárlos rivers, and for carrying the mail from the wharf on the Sarapiquí river to San Juan del Norte and vice versa.

JUAN RAFAEL MORA,
President of the Republic of Costa Rica.

Whereas the Congress has decreed the following:

The Constitutional Congress of the Republic of Costa Rica having considered the contract for *steam navigation on the "Sarapiquí and San Cárlos rivers,"* made by the Supreme Government with the Messrs. Canty on July 8 instant, decrees:

SOLE ARTICLE. The contract for steam navigation upon the Sarapiquí and San Cárlos rivers made by the Supreme Government with the Messrs. Canty is approved, with the exception of Articles VI and VII, which shall read in said contract as follows:

"ARTICLE VI. The Government also grants to the Messrs. Canty a monthly subsidy of $150, in compensation for their services in carrying and bringing the mail, twice a month, between the Sarapiquí wharf and San Juan del Norte."

"ARTICLE VII. Lastly, the Government grants to the Messrs. Canty exemption from taxes on their steamboats, and the protection of the same by the authorities of all ports, as far as is possible."

To the Supreme Executive power.

Given in the Hall of Sessions, in San José, September 23, 1858.

RAFAEL G. ESCALANTE,
President.

JESUS JIMENEZ,
Secretary.

Therefore let it be executed.

National Palace, San José, September 27, 1858.

JUAN RAFAEL MORA.

JOAQUIN BERNARDO CALVO,
Minister of the Interior, Treasury, and War.

No. 42.

Costa Rica is recognized as a party to the canal grant made to Mr. Belly.

JUAN RAFAEL MORA,
President of the Republic of Costa Rica.

Whereas the Constitutional Congress of the Republic having taken into consideration the 28 articles comprised in the Interoceanic Convention, celebrated by the Governments of the Republics of Costa Rica and Nicaragua, with Messrs. Felix Belly and P. M. Milland & Company, of Paris, and considering at the same time the additional article to said convention, has decreed, as follows:

ARTICLE 1. The Interoceanic Convention celebrated between the Governments of the Republics of Costa Rica and Nicaragua and Messrs. Felix Belly and P. M. Milland & Company, of Paris, is approved in all its parts; but with the understanding that the responsibility spoken of in Article 10 shall only apply when the foreign attack or invasion may be lawful.

ARTICLE 2. The present decree shall only have effect after the Congress of the Republic of Nicaragua shall have ratified the Convention, of which reference is made above.

To the Supreme Executive Power.

Given in the Hall of Sessions, in San José, on the 16th day of December, 1858.

RAFAEL G. ESCALANTE,
President.

JESUS JIMENEZ,
Secretary.

MANUEL CASTRO,
Secretary.

Therefore let it be executed.

National Palace, San José, December 16, 1858.

JUAN RAFAEL MORA.

NAZARIO TOLEDO,
Minister of Foreign Relations.

No. 43.

A tax for the benefit of the public instruction of the Province of Guanacaste is levied upon the exportation of wood shipped on the Pacific coast between Cape Blanco and the Gulf of Salinas.

JUAN RAFAEL MORA,
President of the Republic of Costa Rica :

With the view of enlarging the export commerce with the products OF THE IMMENSE FORESTS WHICH THE REPUBLIC POSSESSES IN THE WESTERN PART OF HER TERRITORY, and of providing by this means the Province of Moracia[1] with funds for public instruction, I do hereby decree :

ARTICLE 1. The exportation of crude lumber, of any quality or size, is permitted for the term of five years on any part of the Pacific coast between Cape Blanco and the Gulf of Salinas, without any other duties than those imposed by the present decree.

ARTICLE 2. For each log of wood which, by virtue of the preceding Article, will be shipped from any place on the coast situated in the jurisdiction of the Province of Moracia, the sum of two reals (25 cents) shall be collected, whatever the dimension of the log may be; and the payment shall be made previously to the shipping.

§ 1. The amount of this tax shall be turned over to the fund for public instruction in the Province above named.

§ 2. The Governor of the said Province shall make the collection of this tax by commissioners, whom he shall appoint for that purpose.

ARTICLE 3. Whoever shall ship, or attempt to ship, timber from the places aforesaid, without previously paying the duty prescribed by Article 2d, shall be bound *ipso facto* to pay double.

[1] Guanacaste.

ARTICLE 4. The duty of five cents per cubic foot shall continue to be paid for the timber felled in the littoral of the Gulf of Puntarenas, if the thickness or horizontal section of the log exceeds 12 square inches.

ARTICLE 5. All previous provisions relative to the exportation of timber are hereby repealed.

Given at the National Palace of San José on January 13, 1859.

JUAN RAFAEL MORA.
JOSÉ MARIA CAÑAS,
Secretary of the Treasury.

12

No 44.

New rules enacted in regard to timber within the Zone of the Sarapiquí and other rivers of the Republic on the Atlantic side.

JUAN RAFAEL MORA,
President of the Republic of Costa Rica :

Whereas I have been informed that timber is cut down without permission of the Government on the BANKS OF THE SARAPIQUÍ AND ELSEWHERE IN THE TERRITORY OF THE REPUBLIC ON THE ATLANTIC SIDE, and that in spite of the measures taken by the FRONTIER AUTHORITIES,[1] the said unlawful trade continues, I do hereby decree:

ARTICLE 1. On and after the 1st day of April next it shall be unlawful for any one to cut timber in the territory of the Republic on the Atlantic side, for exportation purposes, without permission of the Executive.

§ 1. In consequence of this provision any one who wishes to engage in this trade, in that section of the country, shall apply to the Executive for a permit, and shall specify in his application the place where he wishes to cut.

§ 2. Before granting the said permit the interested party shall give security for the payment of the duties hereafter to be provided for.

ARTICLE 2. Each log, of whatever thickness, shall be charged the duty of one-half real (6¼ cents) for each yard.

ARTICLE 3. THE MILITARY COMMANDANT OF PUNTA DE CASTILLA,[2] either by himself, or by means of commissioners, shall attend to the collection of this duty, and shall keep for that purpose such books as may be required to show the amount derived from that source.

ARTICLE 4. Whoever, in pursuance of the provisions of this

The new frontier established by the treaty of April 15, 1858.
Eastern extremity of the border line established by the treaty of 1858.

decree, shall engage in the cutting of timber in the places aforesaid, shall be bound, before shipping it, to file before the COMMANDANT OF PUNTA DE CASTILLA a correct bill of lading specifying all the pieces which are to be exported ; and, in case that no such document is filed, or that, if filed, it does not agree with the cargo, he shall pay double duty, and shall forfeit the right to continue cutting timber.

ARTICLE 5. The timber trade which heretofore has been carried on on the *banks of the rivers*[1] *running through the territory of the Republic*, being unlawful, such timber as may be now cut shall not be exported unless with permission of the Government and upon the payment of the duties herein established.

ARTICLE 6. THE COMMANDANTS OF PUNTA DE CASTILLA AND SARAPIQUÍ shall see that this decree is faithfully complied with, and if, as has already happened, their authority is not recognized they shall open an investigation to show that the provisions of this decree have been violated, and shall submit the record thereof with their report to this Department, giving also notice thereof to the General Commandant.

ARTICLE 7. As soon as the General Commandant receives positive information that timber is cut down on the Atlantic side in violation of the present decree, HE SHALL SEND THE PROPER FORCES TO ARREST THE VIOLATORS OF THE LAW OF WHATEVER NATIONALITY THEY MAY BE[2], in order that they may be tried and punished in this Capital according to law. And every settlement or establishment which the violators may have made or erected for the purpose aforesaid, together with tools and all other appurtenances, shall be forfeited.

ARTICLE 8. As soon as the works for the canal through the Nicaraguan Isthmus are undertaken the effect of this decree shall be suspended.[3]

[1] The Sarapiquí, San Cárlos, Rio Frio, and other rivers (treaty of 1858).
[2] Including the neighbor Nicaragua.
[3] This was for the purpose of favoring the enterprise of the canal which always has had the protection of Costa Rica.

Given at the National Palace of San José on March 9, 1859.

JUAN RAFAEL MORA.

JOSÉ MARIA CAÑAS,
Secretary of the Treasury.

No. 45.

Costa Rica approves the contract of interoceanic canal entered into with Mr. Felix Belly, of Paris.

JUAN RAFAEL MORA,
President of the Republic of Costa Rica :

Whereas the Constitutional Congress has decreed as follows :

The Constitutional Congress of the Republic of Costa Rica, upon examination of the amendments made to the international convention RELATIVE TO THE CONSTRUCTION OF A MARITIME INTEROCEANIC CANAL, THROUGH THE SAN JUAN RIVER AND LAKE OF NICARAGUA, ENTERED INTO BETWEEN THE REPUBLICS OF NICARAGUA AND COSTA RICA AND MESSRS. FELIX BELLY & CO., OF PARIS, DECREES :

SOLE ARTICLE. All the amendments made by the Chambers of the Republic of Nicaragua to the Convention above named are hereby approved.

To the Supreme Executive.

Given at the Hall of Sessions at San José, on June 22, 1859.

RAFAEL G. ESCALANTE,
President.

MANUEL CASTRO,
Secretary.

JACINTO TREJOS,
Secretary.

Therefore let it be executed.

National Palace, San José, June 27, 1849.

JUAN RAFAEL MORA.

By sickness of the Hon. Secretary of Foreign Relations,

SALVADOR GONZALEZ,
Assistant Secretary.

No. 46.

Territorial Division of the Republic of Costa Rica for Electoral Purposes, after the treaty of limits of April 15, 1858.

The Senate and the House of Representatives of Costa Rica in Congress assembled, considering that the elections of the supreme officers, and also of the municipal authorities and the juries for press trials, are to be made in accordance with the provisions of the Constitution, have enacted the following law :

TITLE I.—SOLE CHAPTER.

Of the Territorial Division.

ARTICLE 1. The territory of the Republic is divided for electoral purposes into five provinces and one district (comarca), which, in their turn, shall be divided into cantons, and the cantons into districts.

ARTICLE 2. The provinces shall be named San José, Cartago, Heredia, Alajuela and GUANACASTE.

   ＊   ＊   ＊   ＊   ＊   ＊   ＊

ARTICLE 7. THE PROVINCE OF GUANACASTE consists of the city of Liberia (its capital), and of the towns of NICOYA, Santa Cruz, Bagaces, and Cañas. It is divided into four cantons, which shall have the same names as the cities and towns above-mentioned, which shall be the chief towns of the cantons; and the fifth town above-named shall be included in the canton of which the other city immediately preceding it in order is the capital. Each canton shall have two districts.

No. 47.

The Custom Authorities of Costa Rica exercising jurisdiction on the frontier established by the treaty of 1858.

José Maria Montealegre,

President of the Republic of Costa Rica :

Taking into consideration that the revenue interests, both of this Republic and of Nicaragua, demand that some rules should be enacted for the importation and exportation of merchandise through the land frontier between both countries,[1] and as long as a decision completely satisfying this necessity, and made by agreement with the authorities of that Republic is not enacted, I do hereby decree :

Article 1. Whoever shall introduce merchandise in the territory of Costa Rica through the land boundary with Nicaragua shall be bound to obtain a permit to do so from the REVENUE PORT ESTABLISHED ON THE BORDER LINE OF BOTH REPUB-LICS. This permit shall be filed before the Receiver of Public Moneys of Liberia,[2] in order that he may make the liquidation of the duties to be paid therefor according to law.

Article 2. The goods and merchandise introduced in violation of the provisions of the foregoing Article shall be forfeited.

Article 3. The REVENUE POST OF THE FRONTIER shall send a duplicate of the permits issued by it to the Governor of the Province, and the latter shall be bound on his own personal responsibility to transmit those duplicates to the office of the Principal Accountant or Comptroller in order that they may be used to prove the accounts of the Receiver.

Article 4. Whoever shall export, *through the same way,* merchandise destined for the Republic of Nicaragua, shall apply for the proper permit to the Receiver of Public Moneys at Liberia ; and the REVENUE POST OF THE FRONTIER shall detain

---

[1] The new frontier established by the treaty of 1858.
[2] Capital of the Province of Guanacaste.

all merchandise intended to be carried through there, without said permit, until it is duly obtained and filed. The Receiver shall be bound to send a copy of the said permits to the Governor of the Province in order that the latter may transmit them to the principal Treasury authorities in the bordering department of the Republic of Nicaragua.

ARTICLE 5. THE REVENUE POST OF THE FRONTIER shall keep a book wherein all the permits issued by it for the interior of the country shall be copied accurately. And this book shall be sent at the end of every fiscal year to the office of the Comptroller. Another book shall be kept in the same way, wherein all the permits issued by the Receiver of Liberia shall be entered, together with a list of the merchandise exported to Nicaragua; and this shall be sent monthly to the Governor of the Province of Guanacaste for his information.

Given at the National Palace of San José on the 26th day of February, 1861.

> JOSÉ MARIA MONTEALEGRE.
> VICENTE AGUILAR,
> *Secretary of the Treasury.*

No. 48.

Concessions made by Costa Rica for Steam Navigation on the Sarapiqui, San Cárlos, and other rivers tributaries of the San Juan river, and the Lake of Nicaragua, and for the building of a road from the interior of Costa Rica to the Sarapiqui river, or to any other river affluent to the San Juan.

The Senate and House of Representatives of Costa Rica in Congress assembled decree:

ARTICLE 1. The Executive shall inform Messrs. Thomas Horace H. and George Canty that the contracts made on July 8, 1858, for STEAM NAVIGATION ON THE SARAPIQUÍ, SAN CÁRLOS, AND OTHER RIVERS TRIBUTARIES OF THE SAN JUAN RIVER, AND THE LAKE OF NICARAGUA, AND FOR THE BUILDING OF A ROAD FROM THIS CAPITAL TO THE SARAPIQUÍ RIVER, OR TO ANY OTHER EMPTYING INTO THE PORT OF SAN JUAN DEL NORTE, have been terminated.

ARTICLE 2. In case that the company spoken of by Article 1 of the contract for the road, formed within the time stipulated in Article 9 of the same, extended for six months by decree of the provisional Government, and under the conditions established by Article 1 above named, is still in existence, it shall have the power, in spite of the declaration of the preceding Article, to use the right granted to it by Article 12 of the said contract; and in this case the Executive shall have the duty to secure as soon as possible the proper decision.

To the House of Representatives.

Given at the Hall of Sessions at the National Palace, San José, July 31, 1861.

R. RAMIREZ,
President.

JUAN GONZALEZ,
Secretary.

R. FERNANDEZ,
Secretary.

Let it pass to the Executive.

Hall of the House of Representatives in the National Palace, San José. August 5, 1861.

JULIAN VOLIO,
President.

DEMETRIO IGLESIAS,
Secretary.

ANDRES SANCHEZ,
Secretary.

NATIONAL PALACE,
SAN JOSÉ, *August* 12, 1861.

Let it be executed.

JOSÉ MARIA MONTEALEGRE.

FRANCISCO MONTEALEGRE,
Secretary of the Treasury. War, Roads and the Navy.

No. 49.

Municipal territorial division of Costa Rica subsequent to the treaty of limits of 1858.

The Senate and House of Representatives of Costa Rica in Congress assembled, do hereby enact the following municipal ordinance :

SESSION 1ST.

Territorial Division.

ARTICLE 1. The territory of the Republic is divided, for the purposes of municipal administration, into five provinces and one district (comarca), the provinces to be subdivided into cantons, and the cantons into districts.

ARTICLE 2. The provinces shall be named San José, Cartago, Heredia, Alajuela, and GUANACASTE. The comarca shall be named Punta Arenas.

*   *   *   *   *   *

ARTICLE 7. THE PROVINCE OF GUANACASTE consists of the city of Liberia, its capital, and the towns of NICOYA, Santa Cruz, Bagaces, and Cañas. It shall be divided into four cantons, which shall have the same names as the city and towns above mentioned, which shall be their capitals; but the two last-named towns shall form only one canton. Each canton shall be divided into two districts.

No. 50.

Grant made in favor of Don José Antonio Chamorro for the building of a road to the banks of the San Juan river.

The Senate and House of Representatives of Costa Rica in Congress assembled decree :

ARTICLE 1. Permission is hereby given to Don José Antonio Chamorro, as requested by him, to make through the public lands a road to establish communication between the interior of the Republic and *the banks of the San Juan river*, through which cattle proceeding from Nicaragua may be introduced.

*   *   *   *   *   *   *   *

To the Senate.

Given at the Hall of Sessions, National Palace, San José, November 16, 1863.

FRANCISCO M. IGLESIAS,
President.

M. J. ZAMORA,
Secretary.

S. LARA,
Secretary.

To the Executive Power.

Hall of the Senate, National Palace, San José, December 2, 1863.

JOSÉ M. MONTEALEGRE,
President.

JOAQUIN BERNARDO CALVO,
Secretary.

R. FERNANDEZ,
Secretary.

Let it be executed.

JESUS JIMENEZ.

FRANCISCO ECHEVARRIA,
Secretary of the Treasury.

No. 51.

Measures taken in regard to the Guatuso Indians, occupying the plains of the same name in the Rio Frio river in the territorial jurisdiction of the Province of Alajuela, south of the Lake of Nicaragua and the San Juan river.

The Senate and House of Representatives of the Republic of Costa Rica in Congress assembled decree:

ARTICLE 1. The Executive is hereby authorized to appoint those Caciques of Talamanca whom it may choose to select, to be political chiefs of their districts, dependent upon the Governor of the Province of Cartago, and to cause the said Caciques to be paid out of the public Treasury in remuneration of their services, a salary not less than $10 nor more than $20 monthly.

ARTICLE 2. The Executive is also authorized by this decree to appoint a capable and well intentioned person, who with the title of Director of the Talamanca reservation should advise and assist the Caciques in the administration of the Government of the people under them, and suggest such measures as may be conducive to their more speedy civilization, and also furnish such reports and information as the Supreme Government or the Governor of Cartago may ask of him.

ARTICLE 3. As long as the condition of those people does not permit the administration of the Government thereof to be conducted on the same footing as in the rest of the Republic, the Caciques political chiefs shall rule over them, and shall administer justice according to their usages and customs, but subject to the orders of this Government: but it shall never be lawful for them to impose capital punishment, nor the penalty of exile from the territory of the Republic. As to the penalties of imprisonment or confinement at hard labor, they shall have no power to impose them, except for a term not exceeding one year.

ARTICLE 4. An appeal can be taken from the decisions of

the Caciques political chiefs to the Governor of Cartago, and from the decisions of the latter to the President of the Republic; and it shall be their duty, respectively, either to affirm or repeal their decision against which the appeal was taken, according to principles of justice, and upon the proper investigation.

ARTICLE 5. Whenever a person who is not a native of the tribes of Talamanca should be guilty of any grave offense within that jurisdiction, the case shall be properly investigated by the Director, and the record of the investigation shall be sent, together with the accused party, to the Judge for criminal matters of the city of Cartago, where the prisoner shall be tried according to law. The same proceedings shall be resorted to when the culprit is an Indian, and the offense committed by him is a capital one, or is punished by law with expulsion from the territory of the Republic or with the penalties of imprisonment at hard labor for more than one year.

ARTICLE 6. The Executive is hereby authorized to pay a salary which shall not exceed $60 per month to the Curates whom the Bishop of the Diocese should send to those localities, and these Curates, once there, shall not collect fees of any kind.

ARTICLE 7. The Executive is likewise authorized to fix the jurisdictional limits of each political chief, to take all measures conducive to the better administration of the Government of those people, and to appoint such officer as it may deem to be strictly necessary for the service there, and fix their salaries.

ARTICLE 8. *The Executive shall have the power to use the same means as above explained, to undertake the civilization of the Indians called Guatuso Indians, found in the Province of Alajuela, and dependent upon the Governor of the same Province.*

To the House of Representatives.

Given at the Hall of Sessions, National Palace, San José, June 18, 1867.

J. M. MONTEALEGRE,
President.

J. RAFAEL MATA,
Secretary.

RAMON FERNANDEZ,
Secretary.

To the Executive Power.

Hall of the Chamber of Representatives, National Palace, San José, July 24, 1867.

MANUEL A. BONILLA,
President.

ANDRES SAINZ,
Secretary.

JUAN M. CARAZO,
Secretary.

National Palace, San José, July 25, 1867.

Let it be executed.

JOSÉ MARIA CASTRO.

A. ESQUIVEL,
Secretary of the Interior.

No. 52.

Dr. Don Epaminondus Uribe, Commissioner of the Government of Costa Rica, visits the San Juan and San Cárlos rivers, and suggests some measures for the foundation of two Costa Rican towns—one at Punta de Castilla and an other at the confluence of the San Cárlos and the Piñas Blancas rivers.

In compliance with the promise made by us in our former issue, we shall here publish the report made by Don E. Uribe, which we copy from the " Gaceta Oficial " of Costa Rica of July 2. The importance of that report, as far as we are concerned, is to be found especially in what refers to the town of San Juan and the navigability of the Colorado river:

" ALAJUELA, *June* 1, 1868.

" *To the Hon. Secretary of the Interior.*

" SIR : In compliance with the orders that the President of the Republic was pleased to give me to go to SAN JUAN DEL NORTE to examine the condition of its port, of *the road which now is being built from San Ramon to San Cárlos, of the San Cárlos river and of the Colorado river and its bar*, in order to determine whether the said rivers admit of steam navigation, and whether the bar is accessible, and also to find out the proper place to build *a town on the former of the above-said rivers*, and to see how far a steamboat could ascend that stream, *and, finally, to get information whether the authorities of Nicaragua had allowed or abetted the expeditions which some months ago were made by individuals of that Republic against the Guatuso Indians ;*[1] I shall report to you, for the information of the Chief Executive Magistrate, the result of my labors.

_____

[1] Uncivilized Indians who inhabit the plains of the Rio Frio river, south of the Lake of Nicaragua and of the San Juan river.

I left this city on April 4 ultimo, and, passing through the towns of Grecia and San Ramon, I reached San Carlos in fifteen and a half hours (ordinary rate of speed), although the portion of the road between this place and about three leagues beyond San Ramon is the only one which can be called a carriage road. From there I continued my travel through a very narrow path, until the 6th instant; and I did not encounter any other difficulties than the *Catarata Hill* and the Cataract and San Lorenzo rivers, the latter easily admitting of being bridged. As to the hill itself, its difficulties can be lessened by levelling its grade six per cent., and giving to the road the proper windings.

I embarked at the place which is called El Muelle (the wharf), three leagues beyond Peñas Blancas, and although my boat was very heavily laden and it drew two feet of water and the river was very shallow, and we went very slow in order to observe everything well, I reached the San Juan river in twelve hours, without having found in the whole voyage one single place where the water was less than three feet deep, nor any natural obstacle of any kind. I found, however, and this only at certain places, several poles around which sand had accumulated and caused different channels to be formed; but this evil will be very easy to remedy, in my judgment, by removing the said poles, and allowing the water to run from one bank to the other according to the natural inclination of the river bed, and then I think that the depth of the water will not be less than four feet.

As to the San Juan river, I did not find any difficulty in the navigation thereof between the place at which the San Carlos river empties into it and where it branches off to form the Colorado river; but between the latter place and its mouth the boat ran aground several times on account of the shallowness occasioned by the summer season, which, according to the information given by the inhabitants of those localities, had never been so severe before, and also because the Colorado river takes from the San Juan three-quarters of its water.

The Port of San Juan is not at present in good condition because the transit company, owing to the difficulties existing between it and the Government of Nicaragua in regard to a certain contract entered into by them, has completely stopped its work. Nevertheless, I think that this obstacle is not insuperable as far as the interests of the commerce of Costa Rica are concerned, because the only thing to be done in order to obtain that the commerce of Costa Rica be carried on through that place would be to clean, for the distance of one or two miles, that branch of the San Juan river which passes through the grounds of Punta de Castilla, and cause the latter place to communicate, by means of a canal or railroad four miles long, with the fresh-water lake formed by the Colorado river, which lake is three leagues long, two hundred yards wide, and four or five fathoms in depth, and continue from there the navigation through the Colorado river, which at no time of the year lacks five or six feet in depth in either of its branches.

You will understand, sir, and I pray you to call the attention of the President to this point, that these statements are made only through the necessity in which I feel myself in duty bound to report to the Supreme Government all that I have seen and has occurred to me in regard to the subject, which I was directed to investigate, but not by any means because I have the pretension to believe that I have found the philosopher's stone, because I know very well that a matter of such great importance as this cannot be decided authoritatively, except by one who, besides being competent on the subject, would have time and money, neither of which I unfortunately have.

IN REGARD TO THE OBSTACLES APPREHENDED GENERALLY ON ACCOUNT OF THE COMMON RIGHTS OF NICARAGUA AND COSTA RICA IN THE TOWN OF SAN JUAN, OWING TO THE LATTER BEING BUILT ON NICARAGUAN TERRITORY, I BELIEVE THAT THEY WOULD BE OBVIATED SHOULD NOT THE TWO REPUBLICS REACH A SETTLEMENT UPON SOLID GROUNDS, BY PEOPLING PUNTA DE CASTILLA,[1] WHICH

---

[1] Costa Rican territory.

AFFORDS SUFFICIENT EXTENT AND FACILITY, AS WELL AS GOOD
SANITARY CONDITIONS, FOR A VERY GOOD TOWN. UPON THIS SUB-
JECT I AM AUTHORIZED BY SEVERAL MERCHANTS AMONG THE RICH-
EST AND MOST INFLUENTIAL OF SAN JUAN TO SUGGEST TO THE
GOVERNMENT THAT, IF NO ARRANGEMENT CAN BE REACHED WITH
NICARAGUA, THEY WILL MOVE TO THAT PLACE (PUNTA DE
CASTILLA), PROVIDED THAT CERTAIN CONCESSIONS ARE MADE TO
THEM.

As to the point, whether the mouth of the Colorado river is
accessible or not, all that I can say is that, during the twenty-
two days I spent in San Juan, the steamer " Activo " entered
the port on four different occasions, and brought passengers
and cargoes which were transferred to the river boats " Rivas "
and " Panalaya," and carried through the Colorado river without any obstacle to Nicaragua.

Owing to the fact that the Transit Company has suspended
its work I could not obtain a steamboat to ascend the San
Carlos river; but the Captain of the boat " El Cora," who made
that trip last year and went up as far as El Arenal, and four
merchants of respectability, have requested me to petition the
legislative body[1] for the establishment of a line of steamboats in the said river as soon as possible. Nevertheless, in
order to form a correct opinion, even approximately, of what
can be done in this river, I ascended it in a launch of 15 tons
burden, which was laden with a cargo of about 4 tons, and
without having encountered any obstacle I spent four and a
half days in going from the mouth of the San Carlos river
to the wharf.

I examined with care the banks of the San Carlos river between the old wharf and Peñas Blancas, and I think that the
harbor must be located at the confluence, and that the town
must be built upon the angular space formed by the two
rivers, because the ground there is high, level, and extensive
enough.

---

[1] The one of Costa Rica.

I ENDEAVORED AS EARNESTLY AS I COULD TO INVESTIGATE THE PART TAKEN BY THE NICARAGUAN AUTHORITIES IN THE OUTRAGES COMMITTED BY THE CITIZENS OF THAT REPUBLIC AGAINST THE GUATUSO INDIANS,[1] AND I WAS INFORMED BY TRUSTWORTHY PERSONS THAT THE SAID AUTHORITIES, INSTEAD OF FAVORING THE WRONGDOERS, MADE AN EFFORT TO PUNISH THEM.

All that I have said in this report is the result of my own personal observation, and if I succeed in obtaining that my humble work be of any service to the country and satisfactory to the Government you may rest assured that my aspirations will be thoroughly fulfilled.

I have the honor to subscribe myself, your attentive servant,

E. URIBE.

["Gaceta de Nicaragua," 6th year, No. 31, Managua, Saturday, August 1, 1868.]

---

[1] Costa Rican Indians.

No. 53.

The official organ of Nicaragua publishes the estimate of the work to be done on the river and port of San Juan according to surveys made by a mixed commission agreed upon between the Governments of Costa Rica and Nicaragua.

The present step is a forward one made by us on the road of progress. The present administration, following its advanced ideas, directed that a survey of the river and port of San Juan del Norte should be made, in harmony with the Government of Costa Rica, for the purpose of making such improvements as required by the necessities of the commerce of both Republics and the free communication with foreign countries through the Atlantic.

In our preceding issue we published the report of Civil Engineer Don Maximiliano Sonnenstern; and now we print the estimate of the expenses which will be incurred in the work of repairs on the river, port and bay of San Juan, and the measures which are to be taken to render it again freely navigable by steamboats with all safety. The above-named report makes us entertain the hope that the said work so beneficial for the two Republics, necessitating no more expense than $76,000.00, will be easily carried out, and that a new and flattering future will be promised to both countries.

[" Gaceta de Nicaragua " 6th year, No. 46, Managua, November 14, 1868.]

No. 54.

*Editorial of the "Gaceta Oficial" of Nicaragua on the re-
ception in Costa Rica of the Nicaraguan Minister, Don
Mariano Montealegre.—Costa Rica is recognized as bordering upon the San Juan river, as joint possessor of the navigation of the same, and as much interested as Nicaragua in
the Interoceanic Canal enterprise.*

OUR LEGATION IN COSTA RICA.

On the 10th instant, Don Mariano Montealegre, Envoy Extraordinary and Minister Plenipotentiary of Nicaragua, near
the Republic of Costa Rica, was officially received by President Jimenez.

On that occasion the customary speeches were made, the
text of which we print elsewhere.

From the concise and expressive answer of President
Jimenez it is to be concluded that his Government feels well
disposed in regard to the important mission entrusted by Señor
Guzman to Don Mariano Montealegre.

Evidence to the same effect is found in the courteous
manner with which the Costa Rican Government received our
Minister Plenipotentiary. He was not only given the warm-
est reception, but was admitted in the diplomatic body, before
being officially presented to the President, in order that he
could attend the ceremonies of the inauguration of Señor
Jimenez as Chief Magistrate of that Republic.

Nothing else could have been expected, and so we said in
one of our previous numbers (No. 17), from a Magistrate as
the one who now rules the destinies of Costa Rica, and from
the circumstances attending the proclamation of a constitution
as liberal as the one which is now in force in that Republic.

" NICARAGUA AND COSTA RICA," PRESIDENT JIMENEZ SAYS,

" ARE INDEED CALLED BY NATURE TO SHARE RECIPROCALLY THE SAME FATE, AND THEREFORE THEY OUGHT TO STRENGTHEN THEIR FRIENDSHIP, PRESERVE PERFECT HARMONY AND UNITE THEIR EFFORTS TO OPEN FOR THEMSELVES THE PATHS OF COMMON PROGRESS."[1]

These words are indicative of the line of conduct which the Government now established in Costa Rica intends to follow with the rest of the Central American Republics, a line of conduct which is to be hoped will be invariably observed by all the Central American States among themselves,[2] because they all need to preserve their friendship and perfect harmony since their welfare and progress is common.

BUT NICARAGUA AND COSTA RICA, MORE ESPECIALLY STILL, FIND THEMSELVES IN POSITIONS TO STRENGTHEN MORE AND MORE THESE BONDS, AND OF WORKING WITH THE GREATEST EARNESTNESS FOR THE UNITY OF THEIR INTERESTS IN DEFERENCE TO HUMAN PROGRESS, BECAUSE THEY ARE TOPOGRAPHICALLY SITUATED IN THE BEST MANNER POSSIBLE TO ACCOMPLISH THAT PURPOSE.

THE SAN JUAN RIVER, BESIDES DIVIDING THE TERRITORY OF THE TWO STATES,[3] CAUSES THE COMMERCIAL INTERESTS OF BOTH NATIONS TO INTERMIX IN SUCH A WAY THAT NEITHER CAN BE INDIFFERENT TO WHAT HAPPENS IN THAT STREAM.

It has been proved by the most competent experts on the subject, that if ever a port can be opened in this hemisphere to the commerce of the world, by means of a canal uniting the Atlantic with the Pacific Ocean, the only place through which that work can be accomplished is the San Juan river. And this is the reason why our neighbor must not allow the opportunity to pass unnoticed of co-operating in the happiness and progress of Nicaragua BY ACCEPTING THE AYÓN-CHEVALIER CON-

---

[1] In expressing himself in this way the meritorious Don Jesus Jimenez was certainly far from thinking that shortly afterwards his sentiments would find no better return than the denunciation of the treaty of 1858.

[2] The same remark is applicable to these words of the "Gaceta."

[3] Certainly these words are not confirmed by the map appended to the Argument of Nicaragua to which the present is a reply.

TRACT IN THE PART THEREOF WHICH CORRESPONDS TO HER, since in that way she will contribute also to her own happiness and progress.

["Gaceta de Nicaragua," 7th year, No. 21. Managua. Saturday, May 22, 1865].

No. 55.

The exportation through San Juan de Nicaragua of the nat-ural products of the public lands of Costa Rica, such as timber, sarsaparilla, rubber, balsams, resin, &c., is pro-hibited, in order to prevent the natural wealth of the north-ern section of the Republic from being destroyed.[1]

JESUS JIMENEZ,

Provisional President of the Republic of Costa Rica :

In order to prevent the valuable natural productions of the public lands on the Atlantic side from being destroyed, and also to repress smuggling and protect lawful commerce, I do hereby decree :

ARTICLE 1. The exportation THROUGH SAN JUAN DE NICAR-AGUA OF TIMBER, SARSAPARILLA, RUBBER, BALSAMS, RESINS, AND ALL OTHER NATURAL PRODUCTS CUT, OR EXTRACTED, OR COLLECTED, IN THE FORESTS SITUATED ON THE PUBLIC LANDS OF THE REPUBLIC BETWEEN THE ANDES AND THE ATLANTIC, is hereby prohibited, unless under previous authority given by the Judge of the Treasury and by virtue of a contract entered into with the Government by proposals and bids. All works undertaken in the said locality for the purpose of exporting the said products in the manner aforesaid are also prohibited.

ARTICLE 2. Whoever shall violate the provisions of the foregoing Article shall lose the cargo so attempted to be carried and shall be fined one hundred dollars, or, in default of pay-ment, if the person has not sufficient property within the Re-public to pay that amount, he shall suffer three months of im-prisonment at hard labor.

ARTICLE 3. REVENUE POSTS SHALL BE ESTABLISHED IN EVERY PLACE OF CONFLUENCE OF THE SAN CÁRLOS AND SARAPIQUÍ RIVERS WITH THE SAN JUAN. Each one of these posts shall be commanded by a corporal, who shall have three privates under him; but the number of the latter shall be increased if the

---

[1] This decree was the first germ of the idea of repudiating the treaty of 1851.

necessities of the service require it. The corporals shall be paid fifty dollars and the guards thirty-five dollars per month each.

ARTICLE 4. It shall be the duty of these posts, 1st. To prevent the exportation of the natural products of the public lands of the Republic, and their being worked or obtained for that purpose. 2d. To seize those products already cut down, collected or extracted, and send them whenever possible and convenient, together with the arrested transgressors, to the nearest authority in order that the latter may cause the preliminary investigation to be made and submit the record thereof, together with the prisoners, to the court which must pass sentence. 3d. To seize every article the trade of which the Government has reserved for itself and those whose importation is forbidden, if attempted to be introduced into the Republic, and send them, together with the prisoners, to the nearest authority, in the manner and for the purposes above named.' And 4th. To watch that no articles of lawful commerce are introduced into the country without the formalities prescribed by this decree; to detain those which may be attempted to be introduced clandestinely and fraudulently; and to report without loss of time to the proper officer, who must declare them forfeited.

　　　*　　　*　　　*　　　*　　　*　　　*

ARTICLE 16. Whoever shall be arrested while making or assisting in the exportation of the natural products aforesaid without the proper authority and without paying the duties established, shall be punished according to the provisions of Article 2 of the present decree; but if it should be found out that he has already made the exportation then he shall have to pay a double fine or to undergo double time in prison at hard labor, whatever the nature and quantity of the exported articles may be.

Given at the National Palace at San José on April 28, 1869.

JESUS JIMENEZ.

JUAN RAFAEL MATA,

Secretary of the Treasury.

No. 56.

The territorial jurisdiction of the " Comarca " (District) of Limon is created.—The limits given to it are from Punta de Castilla, frontier of Nicaragua, to the United States of Colombia.

The Provisional Chief Magistrate of the Republic, taking into consideration the distance which separates the people of the northern section of the Republic from this capital, and the peculiar necessities of those scattered villages, does hereby decree :

Article 1. The towns and villages in the Valley of Matina, and along the whole northern littoral of the Republic, from Punta de Castilla, which is the limit of Nicaragua,[1] down to the frontiers of the United States of Colombia, are hereby declared to constitute, for all purposes of Government, the Comarca or District of Limon, whose capital shall be the village of Moin, where the officers exercising jurisdiction in the whole territory of the comarca shall establish their residence.

Article 2. The Government of the comarca shall be administered in the following way :

There shall be a Governor, with the functions and powers given by law to the provincial Governors.

There shall be one constitutional Alcalde, exercising the authority given to the officers of this kind by the laws of the country.

There shall be as many justices of the peace as are now, or may in the future be established, according to law, in the towns or villages and districts belonging to the comarca, and the territorial limits within which they shall exercise jurisdiction shall be fixed, as far as possible, by the Governor.

There shall also be a military commandant and a harbor-master.

[1] Treaty of 1858.

The municipal authority shall be vested in the Governor, as provided for by law in regard to the comarca of Punta Arenas.

ARTICLE 3. In judicial matters, the comarca shall be submitted to the jurisdiction of the courts of first instance of the province of Cartago.

ARTICLE 4. For electoral purposes, the comarca shall be considered as a district annexed to the canton of El Paraiso, in the above-named province of Cartago.

Given at the National Palace, on June 6, 1870.

BRUNO CARRANZA.

JOAQUIN LIZANO,

Secretary of the Interior.

No. 57.

Origin of the Martinez-Jerez Duumvirate.

[From Memorias para la historia de la campaña nacional contra el filibusterismo, 1856, y 57 por Jerónimo Perez. Masaya, 1874.]

MARTINEZ AND JEREZ.

Legitimists and Democrats thought that the continuation of the civil war was inevitable, for which reason several leaders who had been impressed by the danger run during the late national war, endeavored to bring about some understanding between the heads of the two parties. We have a letter of General Chamorro wherein he said to Martinez: "*It is necessary for you and for Jerez, as the two men of most prestige, to take upon yourselves the task of constituting the Republic, and overcome the difficult situation subsequent to Walker's downfall.*"

The two leaders, with a portion of their forces, embarked on the steamer San Cárlos and landed at Granada, where Martinez remained. Jerez reached Leon, receiving the ovations of the whole people. General Barrios placed upon his head a wreath of laurels.

Martinez, with several orientals, and Jerez, with several occidentals, assembled at Managua, endeavored in vain to make an arrangement. They were about to take leave of each other to commence again the fratricidal struggle, when Jerez, in company with Don Evaristo Carazo, went to the rooms of Martinez, who happened to be in company with Don Ignacio Padilla and the author of these Memoirs, and said to him: "*Do you wish you and me to assume the power and to govern the Republic dictatorially until the country is reorganized by us?*" Yes, I will, was the answer. And an agreement was drawn up and signed establishing the Duumvirate, which, in spite of all the predictions to the contrary, not only saved the country from the new struggle which threatened it, but wisely conducted it to its constitutional organization.

CHRONOLOGICAL EPITOME

COSTA RICA AND NICARAGUA.

1502.—Fourth voyage of Columbus. Discovery of the eastern coast of Central America, from Cape Honduras down to Portobello and Cape Marmol, embracing the ancient Province of Veragua.

1509.—The King of Spain erects the Governorship of VERAGUA in favor of Diego de Nicuesa, from Cape Gracias á Dios to the Gulf of Darien.

1513.—Discovery of the Pacific Ocean or Southern Sea by Vasco Nuñez de Balboa.

1514.—Pedrarias Dávila, Governor of CASTILLA DEL ORO, lands at Darien.

1519.—15th August. Panamá founded.

1519.—Discovery of BURICA, Gulf of Osa (now Golfo Dulce, Costa-Rica), and Gulf of Nicoya.

1520.—Natá founded.

1521.—6th September. Royal ordinance (Real Cédula) fixing the boundaries of Panamá or Governorship of Castilla del Oro, its western limit being the Province of Veragua.

1522.—Discovery of NICARAGUA, on the Southern Sea, by Gil Gonzalez Dávila.

1524.—Conquest of Nicaragua by Francisco Hernandez de Córdoba. The cities of Leon and Granada founded.

1525.—First survey of Lake Nicaragua by Captain Ruy Diaz, who discovers its egress or outlet, el Desaguadero.

1525.—Hernando de Soto surveys the upper part of the Desaguadero, from the lake to the first rapid, near the

Indian settlement of *Voto*, on the right or Costa-Rican bank of the river.

1526.—Pedrarias Dávila leaves Panamá and comes to Nicaragua to quell the rebellion of his lieutenant Francisco Hernandez de Córdoba. Córdoba is tried and put to death.

1527.—Pedrarias Dávila is superseded as Governor of Castilla del Oro by Pedro de los Rios and is appointed Governor and Captain-General of NICARAGUA. No boundaries were fixed to this Government, which was to embrace the lands conquered by Francisco Hernandez de Córdoba on the Southern Sea.

1529.—Pedrarias Dávila sends Martin Estete on a surveying expedition to the DESAGUADERO. Estete goes no farther than Captains Ruy Diaz and Hernando de Soto, but he lands at Voto and explores Costa Rica up to the Suerre river. Gabriel de Rojas, Hernan Sanchez de Badajoz, Diego de Castañeda, &c., were the principal captains of this campaign.

1534.—4th May. Rodrigo de Contreras is appointed Governor and Captain-General of Nicaragua, in the same manner as Pedrarias Dávila. No boundaries were marked and Nicaragua remains confined to the Southern Sea.

1534.—December 24. Felipe Gutierrez is appointed Governor of the Province of VERAGUA, under reservation of the rights of Columbus's heirs, his jurisdiction extending from Cape Gracias á Dios down to Castilla del Oro.

1537.—Creation of the DUKEDOM OF VERAGUA, in favor of Don Luis Colon, grandson of Columbus. This Dukedom comprised, from sea to sea, 25 square leagues, between Chiriquí Lagoon (Zarabaro Bay) and River Belen. The Province of Veragua (Costa Rica) granted to Felipe Gutierrez was thenceforth bounded by the Dukedom of the same name to the southeast and by Cape Gracias á Dios to the north, including the whole Mosquito coast, the rivers Yare, Caxines (Escondido), San Juan, Suerre, &c., within the jurisdiction of Veragua.

1539.—Captains Alonso Calero and Diego Machuca survey the DESAGUADERO and sail from Lake Nicaragua to the sea.

1539.—Hernan Sanchez de Badajoz is appointed Governor of Costa Rica, or Veragua, to succeed Felipe Gutierrez.

1540.—April. Hernan Sanchez de Badajoz lands at the mouth of the Rio Tarire (Sixola or Tiliri river) and founds the first Spanish settlement on the northern coast of Costa Rica. The King of Spain did not approve the commission of Hernan Sanchez de Badajoz.

1540.—November 29th. Diego Gutierrez, Felipe's brother, is appointed Governor of *Veragua*, New Cartago or Costa Rica. This Province, which, under Felipe, ended at Cape Gracias á Dios, was enlarged northwards farther than Cape Camaron to the banks of the Rio Grande (River Aguan or Roman). Its southern limit was the Dukedom of Veragua.

1540. From this date the *ducal estate* of Veragua was called by this name, and the *royal province* of Veragua was named *Cartago* or *Costa Rica*.

1556.—The Dukedom of Veragua reverts to the Royal Crown, and is incorporated into the Royal domain.

1560-1573—NUEVO CARTAGO or COSTA RICA, comprising the territory of the Desaguadero, is conquered, settled, and governed in succession by Juan Cavallon, Juan Vazquez de Coronado, Perafán de Ribera.

1572.—Perafán de Ribera, Governor of Costa Rica, is appointed Corregidor of Nicoya.

1573.—December 1st.—Philip II appoints Diego de Artieda Governor and Captain-General of Costa Rica, and marks the boundaries of this Province, as follows:

In latitude, from sea to sea ; and in longitude on the Caribbean Sea, from the San Juan river, the main outlet or Desagnadero of Lake Nicaragua, to the confines of Veragua (the Escudo de Veragua), and on the Southern Sea, from the limits of Nicoya to the valleys of Chiriqui (River Chiriqui Viejo).

1573.—Diego de Artieda is appointed Governor of Nicoya.

1576.—The early Province of Nuevo Cartago or Costa Rica reduced to the boundaries marked by Philip II in 1573. A new province was created to the north of the Desagnadero, called the Province of Taguzgalpa. Its limits were from the northern mouth of the San Juan river alongside the coast to Cape Camaron, and all the land between the sea and the boundary line of Nicaragua, Nueva Segovia, and Honduras.

The jurisdiction of Nicaragua did not go beyond fifteen leagues from the lake shore to the east. It is plain by the demarcation of Costa Rica in 1573, and by that of Taguzgalpa in 1576, giving to these Provinces the full jurisdiction on the Desaguadero from its mouths to fifteen leagues from the lake, that Nicaragua did not possess an inch of territory on the Caribbean Sea, at the end of the XVIth century, when the territorial status of the Audiencia of Guatemala was finally regulated.

The Taguzgalpa or Mosquito coast, from 1509 to 1573, a part of Veragua, Nuevo Cartago, or Costa Rica, remained unsettled and open to piratical invasions during the XVIIth century. The English settled at Rio Tinto (Black River), Cape Gracias á Dios and Bluefields, or afforded protection to the Mosquito Indians.

By the treaty of Versailles of 1783 between Spain and England, this latter Power agreed to evacuate the settlements aforesaid. A more comprehensive and precise engagement was entered into by the additional treaty of London of 1786 between the same parties. England was compelled to evacuate the Mosquito coast ; but she did not give up the hope of having

14

a permanent footing there, and, though apparently complying with her treaty obligations, she devised means to elude them practically, and encouraged some private individuals to submit to the Spanish law, to become Spanish subjects, and to ask grants of lands, &c. This was the case with Col. Robert Hodgson, to whose endeavors the Mosquito protectorate of modern times owes filial regard. Spain, however, recovered the control of the Mosquito coast which was placed directly under the military supervision of the Captain-General of Guatemala.

ERRATA.

Page.	Line.	Reads	Should Read
iv	16	Tausgalpa	Taguzgalpa
27	29	San Cárlos	San Carlos
And wherever else found.			
51	4	1828	1826
66	5	fory	for
97	4	place	placed
103	8	May, 1813	1812
110	27	Escacú	Escasú
"	"	"	"
"	31	Cucurrique	Tucurrique
117	17	the	an
"	25	FRARJANES	FRAIJANES
"	27	BLASCO	BLANCO
119	25	1881	1831
134	12	Totogalpa	Tologalpa
"	21	Gorge	Jorge
164	2	*Sarapiqui*	*Sarapiqui*
167	8	1858	1838
171	9	Posaltega	Posoltega
"	10	Posaltegüilla	Posolteguilla
172	25	San Gorge	San Jorge
181	26	1849	1859

www.ingramcontent.com/pod-product-compliance
Lightning Source LLC
Chambersburg PA
CBHW030323270326
41926CB00010B/1481